THE EVOLUTION OF MAN AND THE MODERN SOCIETY IN MOUNTAINOUS SIKKIM

THE EVOLUTION OF MAN AND THE MODERN SOCIETY IN MOUNTAINOUS SIKKIM

J.R. Subba

GYAN PUBLISHING HOUSE
NEW DELHI-110002

The Evolution of Man and the Modern Society in Mountainous Sikkim

Rs. 360

ISBN 978-81-212-1009-6

Published in 2008 in India by
Gyan Publishing House,
23 Main Ansari Road Darya Ganj
New Delhi-110002
Phones : 23282060, 23261060
Fax : (011) 23285914
E-mail: gyanbooks@vsnl.com
Website : http : // www.gyanbooks.com

Laser Typesetting by : Quick Media, Delhi
Printed at : Singhal Print Media, Delhi

Contents

Foreword

This book, titled "The Evolution of Man and the Modern Society in Mountainous Sikkim" written by J.R. Subba, is an interesting reading. It is evident from the writing of Mr. Subba that he is interested in human bio-cultural history in an evolutionary perspective. He has written many books on Sikkim, but this one has been done on a different idea, altogether. This book considers human phenomenon on a global scale, but considers local scenario, as a part of the whole.

He has chosen five chapters in this book with topics ranging from mega evolutionary history of man, along with three other important human cultural attributes viz. food production, writing system and developmental stages of human society, and finally sustainability issues of Sikkimese population. Although he made an attempt to portray global scenario pertaining to the chosen topics in first four chapters, his focus was retained on the Sikkim Himalayan specifics. The last chapter, however, was purportedly designed for the Sikkim Himalaya, as a representative locale of the Hindu-Kush Himalaya in terms of a sustainable developmental model. Overall, placing Sikkimese population and its society in the realm of evolutionary paradigm has been the goal of this book.

Human evolution, both at macro- and micro-level, has been an important topic of study for long. Over the last 100 years, several developments, both theoretical and methodological, added new dimensions in the study of human evolutionary history. Furthermore, the study of human biological diversity has been enormously challenging and historically been controversial. In this book, Mr. Subba tried to enrich the readers on important points of human evolution.

Food production, including maintenance of livestock is one of the essential features of bio-cultural survival for majority of global human populations. Understanding the evolutionary aspects of food production and livestock rearing takes us back to the era of domestication of wild plants and animals. The fascinating saga pertaining to evolution from hunter-gatherers to food producers tells us about the techno-ecological adaptations of humans in an evolutionary sense. Mr. Subba made an attempt to place before the readers a profile of evolutionary history of food production, considering both global and local levels.

It is true to note that the history of progression of human beings from hunter-gathering (savagery) to civilization include the development of agriculture, metallurgy, complex technology and writing system. The evolutionary aspects of the writing systems and its variations, the world over has been dealt with by Mr. Subba in this book Particular detailed discussion on the writing systems of various populations of Sikkim is thoroughly informative.

The evolutionary aspects of human society are an exceptionally interesting topic in the domain of social sciences. It depicts the human-environment interactions in time and space. It also clearly portrays the adaptive significance of these interactions. This book puts emphasis to the history of development of human society in an evolutionary framework. It is done for Indian society in general, and Sikkimese society in particular. The task to describe and analyze social development is a challenging one and Mr. Subba has done a praiseworthy job.

The final chapter deals with a discussion on a project findings and recommendations concerning sustainable livelihood issues of the population of Sikkim. The discussion has found a place in this book, to my understanding, owing to the importance of the issue in the present day modern Sikkim. A fragile mountainous environment demands very cautious steps in the matters of economic choices of people. Sustainable livelihood options, therefore, becomes a genuine necessity. The thorough analysis and interpretations of the available data on agri-horticultural practices of the state, and viability and sustainability aspects of such practices deserves appreciation.

This book, I believe, will be liked by those who want to know on human phenomenon in general, and development of human societies in Sikkim, in particular.

Barun Mukhopadhyay, Ph.D.
Professor-in-Charge
Biological Sciences Division
Indian Statistical Institute
Kolkata

Preface

Charles Darwin was the first man to suggest and prove through evidence collected from fossils that all species had evolved. Next, it was T. H. Huxley who publicly associated humans with apes. Human fossils worked a special magic in the history of scientific evolution study of mankind.

The first chapter examines the fossil evidences of human evolution and their spread around the world. The modern thinking man evolved 50,000 years ago, but his ancestors (*Austrolopithecus afarensis*) started walking upright between 3 and 4 million years ago in the forest; started using stone tools about 2.5 million years ago (*Homo habilis*). However, not much of the evolutionary history of modern man between 50,000 to 11,000 years ago is known so far.

The second chapter provides insight into the evolutionary history of food production by the modern thinking man. The end of the Pleistocene Era and last Ice Age correspond approximately to 11,000 B.C. which marks the beginning of village life in a few parts of the world. The modern man learnt food production by domestication of wild plants 11,000 years ago, first in the Fertile Crescent in Southwest Asia (8,000 B.C.), then in China (7,500 B.C.), in Sahel (5,000 B.C.) and in Mesoamerica (3,000 B.C.). Thereafter, agriculture spread around the world. Similarly, domestication of wild animals also started in the Fertile Crescent; sheep and goat (8,000 B.C.), cow (6,000 B.C.), pig (8,000 B.C.) in China, Horse (4,000 B.C.), and so on. Slowly, the modern man started depending on agriculture for food, and gave up hunting and gathering life style in most parts of the world.

The third chapter illustrates in brief, the evolutionary history of writing systems. The Sumerians of Mesopotamia (before 3,000 B.C.), China (2,800 B.C.), and Mexican Indians (600 B.C.), were the undisputed centres of independent inventions of writing systems. The Alphabet was devised in Egypt around 2,000 B.C. but the Semites were the actual inventors of alphabets about 1700 B.C. The alphabetic writing systems then spread around the world through blueprint copying and idea diffusion thereafter.

In India, picto-phonographic script was developed during Indus Valley Civilization (2,600 - 1,700 B.C.) that lasted for about 1,900 years in the civilization of Dravidians. Historians believe that from this, the Proto-Brahmi script was developed by 1,000 B.C. Based on this Proto-Brahmi script, the Dravidians of South Indian developed the South Indian Brahmi by 800 B.C. Similarly, after the Aryans came to India, they also developed North India Brahmi from the same Proto-Brahmi script probably around the same period. By the time of Emperor Ashọka (272-232 B.C.), Brahmi script was well developed in India. Later, a number of regional scripts were developed for the regional languages of India and abroad from the Brahmi script of Ashoka and Gupta's period.

The fourth chapter delves into the evolution history of modern society. Probably, all humans lived in bands untill atleast 40,000 years ago, and most still did till as recently as 11,000 years ago. Tribal organizations began to emerge about 13,000 years ago for the first time in the Fertile Crescent. Later, tribal organization spread in other areas of the world, and in mountainous Sikkim only by 7th century A.D. Chiefdoms arose by 5,500 B.C. in the Fertile Crescent, in Mesoamerica by 1,000 B.C., and in Sikkim by 1642 A. D. States arose around 3,700 B.C. in Mesopotamia, around 300 B.C. in Mesoamerica, over 2,000 years ago in the Andes,

China and Southeast Asia including India, and in Sikkim by 1975 A.D.

The fifth chapter summarizes briefly the SARD-M (Sustainable Agriculture and Rural Development in Mountainous Region) Policy Assessments for mountainous Sikkim. The Policy Assessment study was a part of a three-year Project (2005-07) led by the FAO (Food and Agriculture Organization), Rome, and participated in by ICIMOD (International Centre for Integrated Mountain Development), Kathmandu, Nepal. I was involved for this study project as Consultant in India (Sikkim). The study aims to support the rural livelihoods of mountain peoples by facilitating the design, review, implementation and evolution of relevant policy packages and institutional processes promoting SARD in mountain region. The study examines the strengths and weaknesses of SARD-M policies, provide technological framework or guidelines for appropriate steps of interventions and suggests to overcome weaknesses for sustainable agriculture and rural development in mountainous Sikkim

J.R. Subba

Acknowledgements

I am extremely grateful to those who helped me on various aspects of study while preparing the manuscript for this book, especially, Dr. E. Sharma, Dr. P. Gyamtsho, and Dr. N.S. Jodha of ICIMOD, Kathmandu, Nepal; Dr. Takashi Takahatake, FAO, Rome, and various Sikkim Government Departmental Heads and officials for SARD-M Policy Assessment Study in India (Sikkim).

I am thankful to Shri P. K. Chamling, the Hon'ble Chief Minister of Sikkim and Shri Somnath Poudyal, Hon'ble Minister Agriculture and Horticulture for allowing me to accept the consultancy work for SARD-M in India (Sikkim) during 2005-2007.

I also extend my grateful thanks to all the learned scholars, whose works I have consulted and referred to in this book.

I acknowledge my thanks to Mr. Pema Wanchuk, Editor, Now, News Paper, Gantok, Sikkim for going through the manuscript; and Mr. Dependra Dewan and Mrs. Sheela Thami Dahal, Himadri Printers, NamNang, Gantok for laser type setting.

Lastly, I am also extremely thankful to Dr. Barun Mukhopadhyay, Ph.D. Professor-in-Charge.Biological Sciences Division, Indian Statistical Institute, Kolkata for writing a befitting foreword.

J. R. Subba

1
The Human Evolution

On September 1, 2007, I happened to visit the World Tour Exhibition of Lucy – the Plio-Pleistocene hominid fossil, the ancestor of humankind discovered at Hadar in Ethiopia by Johanson, D. C. and White, T. M. in 1976. The experts at the Natural Science Museum, Houston, USA, where the exhibition was being held told me three things about Lucy:

(i) Lucy is different from all other fossils discovered and named thus far. She is very old, very primitive, a very small hominid, and named *Australopithecus afarensis*.

(ii) It is her completeness [40% of the fossil bones recovered] that makes her unique. Until she was found, there weren't any very old and complete skeletons. The oldest till Lucy was Neanderthal remains, barely 75,000 years old. Neanderthals disappeared with the appearance of the Cro-Magnon "cave man" which arrived 40,000 – 50,000 years back and may have disappeared as recently as 10,000 years ago. The cavemen were men like us. Yes, there are older hominid fossils discovered, but they are all fragments. Everything that has been reconstructed from them has had to be done by matching up those little pieces – a tooth here, a bit of jaw there, may be a complete skull from some where else, plus a leg bone from some other place.

(iii) Lucy is approximately 3.5 million years old. She is the oldest, most complete, best-preserved skeleton of any erect-walking human ancestor that has ever been found.

All human beings are hominids, but not all hominids are human beings. The paleoanthropologists can picture human evolution as starting with a primitive apelike type that gradually, over a long period of time, became less and less apelike and more manlike. There was no abrupt crossover from ape to human, but probably a rather fuzzy time of in-between types that would be difficult to classify either way. We have no fossils yet that tell us what went on during that in-between time. Therefore, the handiest way of separating the newer types from their ape ancestors is to lump together all those that stood up on their hind legs and became bipedal. That group of men and near-men is called hominid.

The paleoanthropologists have studied the evolution of species. They found that descent, and lines of related species could be traced in fossils. The fossils with which Darwin chose to back up his "The Origin of Species" theory were as uncontroversial as he could make them: obscure marine organisms, small branacles, long-extinct clams, and so on.

Now, based on the evidence of the fossils of species collected from various places around the world, the paleoanthropologists have studied biostratigraphic evidence of living species and divided the Living-World into three broad Eras; Viz:

(a) Paleozoic Era of antiquity to 230 million years before the present,
(b) Mesozoic Era of 230 to 63 million years before the present; and
(c) Cenozoic Era of 63 millions of years before to the present. Each Era has been further divided into different periods. The sequence of evolution of living species of the world could be summarised as follows:

a) Paleozoic Era (? to 230 million years before the present):

(i) Prior to the Cambrian period (600-500 million years before the present), only single-celled and small multi-celled forms such as bacteria, algae, fungi and small, soft-bodied marine animals were living in this world.
(ii) Trilobites, worms, sponges and early mollusks appeared in the sea during the Cambrian period (600-500 million years).
(iii) Primitive fish, clams, starfish, corals, and seaweeds evolved during Ordovician period (500-425 million years).
(iv) First land plants, scorpions and millipedes appeared on land in the Silurian period (425-405 million years).

(v) First large treelike land plants, many sea vertebrates and first amphibians appeared in the Devonian period (405-345 million years).

(vi) Giant primitive insects on land and first reptiles appeared in the Carboniferous period (345-280 million years). Fish fauna also flourished.

(vii) First modern insects appearance and development of amphibians and reptiles occurred during the Permian period (280-230 million years). Fish fauna proliferated in the sea but trilobites became extinct during this period.

(b) Mesozoic Era (230 to 63 million years before):

(viii) First dinosaurs appear, and the appearance of lobsters and other arthropods in sea marked the Triassic period (230-181 million years).

(ix) The Jurassic period (181 –135 million years) marks the appearance of first true mammals and birds. Dinosaurs were at their peak during this period.

(x) Dinosaurs become extinct in the Cretaceous period (135-63 million years). Great increase in numbers of small mammals; and hard wood forests with large modern trees appeared during this period.

(c) Cenozoic Era (63 to 0 million years before):

(xi) The Tertiary and Quaternary period (63-0 million years) are marked by the first appearance of prosimians and large mammals which begin to dominate land. Bony fish become abundant in sea; and appearance of sharks.

Further, the paleoanthropologists have divided the last quarter of the Cenozoic Era to the present (25 to 0 million years before) into three categories Viz: (a) Miocene (25 – 5 million years before the present); (b) Pliocene (5 – 2 million years before the present) and, (c) Pleistocene (2 – 1 million years before the present).

(a) Miocene (25 – 5 million years before the present):

Prior to 25 million years, proto-monkeys and proto-apes – the ancestors of modern apes and monkeys evolved from more primitive prosimian forms. Miocene apes evolved about twenty million years back. One of the earliest forms known is the *Dryopithecus africanus* (also known as *Procosul* after a captive ape that lived in the London Zoo), found by Louis Leakey at Lake Victoria. Other

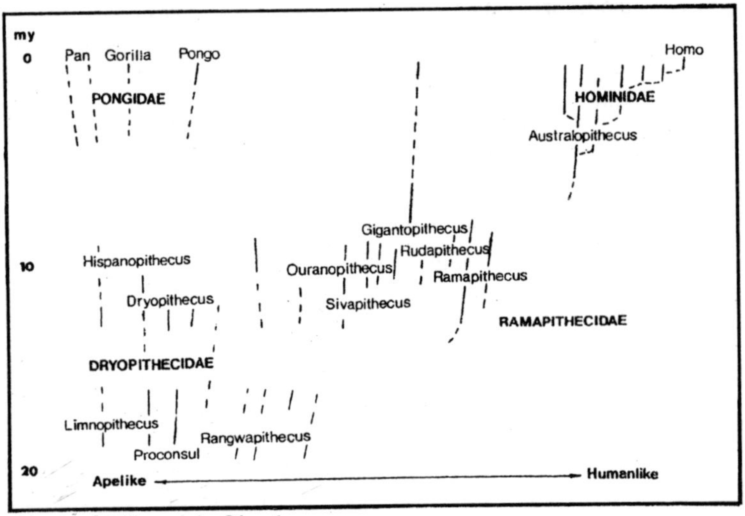

Source: Pilbeam's Chart

Dryopithecus-like forms turn up in later millennia, sprinkled down through eighteen and seventeen million all the way to about nine million years ago. They existed in several shapes and sizes, and were scattered widely in Africa, in central and southern Europe, and in Asia. Like all apes, they frequented forests, and their distribution follows the range of the great tropical forest belt that girdled the earth at the beginning of the Miocene. The most recent attempt to sort out the confusing Miocene ape tangle was made by David Pilbeam. Pilbeam, a pioneer scientist of Miocene apes, in his twenty years of study lumped the several forms of Miocene apes into a family – the Dryopithecids and Ramapithecids. He placed *Limnopithecus* at the extreme left of his chart in his plain arrangement because it is the most apelike of the Miocene types. *Ramapithecus* was a very small form, no larger than a medium-sized dog, at 30 lbs. or so, collected from India, Pakistan and Europe.

It was not a biped but an agile four-footed animal perhaps equally at home in the trees as on the ground. It probably used tools with no greater proficiency that the chimpanzee does nowadays.

Pilbeam divided these fossils into two major groups: the Dryopithecidae - those that do not have hominid dentition and were presumably ancestral to modern apes, and the Ramapithecidae - those whose dentition have hominid traits. Of the latter, *Ramapithecus* is considered the most humanlike; therefore it is farthest to the right on Pilbeam's chart. The true hominids are placed even farther to the right, and there is a large gap between them and *Ramapithecus*.

Fossils of another giant Miocene ape, the *Gigantopithecus*, were collected from Pakistan and India. These were about nine million years old. The *Gigantopithecus* (not a human ancestor) went extinct as recently as half a million years ago in China. Of the others, *Sivapithecus* medium size ape fossil collected from Pakistan is now the best represented with more than sixty fossil pieces, jaws and teeth recovered to date. It is possibly more terrestrial than a chimp.

(b) Pliocene (5 to 2 million years before the present):

The Hominid fossils of *Australopithecus afarensis* from Hadar, Ethiopia, *Austrelopithecus afarensis* from Laetopli, Nairobi, Hominid fossils of Kanapoi, and *Australopithecus africanus* from South Africa represent the period of Pliocene period (5 to 2 million years).

(c) Pleistocene (2 to 0.01 million years before the present):

The Hominid fossils of *Australopithecus africanus* and *Austrelopithcus robustus* from Omo, Turkana, Olduvai, South Africa, *Homo habilis* from Turkana, Olduvai, *Homo erectus* from Turkana, Olduvai, *Homo erectus* from throughout the world, and *Homo sapiens neanderthalensis* and *Homo sapiens sapiens* from Old and New Worlds represent the period of Pleistocene.

Paleoanthropologists hold that our closest living relatives are the three surviving species of the great ape: the gorilla, the common chimpanzee, and the pigmy chimpanzee (bonobo). Their confinement to Africa, along with abundant fossil evidence, indicates that the earliest stages of human evolution also played out in Africa. Human history, as something separate from the history of animals, began here about 5 to 9 million years ago, as the discovery of *Ramapithecus, Shivapithecus* etc. types of hominids in Europe, Pakistan and India suggest. Around that time, a population of African apes broke up into several populations, one of which proceeded to evolve into modern gorillas, a second into the two chimps, and the third into humans. The gorilla line apparently split off slightly before the split between the chimp and the human lines. Fossils indicate that the evolutionary line leading to humans achieved a substantially upright posture 4 to 3.5 million years ago, a population now known as *Australopithecus afarensis* (example is Lucy). Then *A. afarensis* population began to increase in body size and in relation to brain-size around 2.7 to 2.2 million years ago. Those proto-humans are generally known as *Australopithecus afarensis, Homo habilis, Homo erectus*. The fossils indicate that *A. afarensis* broke up into several populations of two lines, one leading to "gracile" types hominid *A. africanus* between 2.7 to 2.2 million; and then evolved into a population of "robust" type hominid *A. robustus* with larger mandibles and larger molars between 2.1 to 1 million years ago. These became extinct a million years ago. The line is known as australopithecines and they are not our ancestors.

The other line evolved into several populations of *Homo habilis* with larger front teeth between 2.3 to 1.8 million and evolved into several populations of *Homo erectus* with larger body size, shape and larger brain between 2.0 to 1.5 million years ago. *Homo erectus* evolved into several populations of *Homo sapiens neaderthalensis* between 2.0 to 0.5 million and the modern thinking man *Homo sapiens sapeins* by 50,000-40,000 years ago. They are our ancestors. The paleoanthropologists have described the fossil evidences of human evolution in detail as follows:

1. The Early Fossil Discoveries

Man has always been more interested in his own origins; he traces his family roots and takes pride in their length. He follows the histories of nations to his own roots. He looks behind recorded history to the beginnings of civilizations, and ultimately to the beginnings of humanity itself. Where he comes from is what interests him most. Human fossils thus work a special magic for him.

Charles Darwin was the first person to indicate and prove through fossil evidence that all species had evolved. He also hinted that evolution had something to do with humans as they are now; "Light will be thrown on the origin of man and his history" (Charles, Darwin, 1964). It was T. H. Huxley who publicly associated humans with apes. He pointed out the great range of similarities between man and what he recognized to be man's closest living relatives, the gorilla and the chimpanzee. From this, he reasoned that the three had a common and not extremely remote ancestor. Since these apes were found only in Africa, Huxley suggested that fossils of the joint ancestor might also be found there. Unfortunately, no known fossil ancestors had been found in Africa till that time.

A great deal of this basic spadework was done in the latter half of the nineteenth century. In 1891, a Dutch scientist, Eugene Dubois found parts of a skull and a leg bone in a Solo riverbank in Java. The great age of his finds, an estimated half-a million-years-old, and its extremely primitive appearance caused it to be viewed with great suspicion. He named his find *Pithecanthus erectus*. Meanwhile, German paleontologists Rudolf Virchow and Sir Arthur Keith's group accumulated new evidence. Heidelberg Man, represented by a heavy apelike jaw containing manlike teeth, was discovered in a commercial sandpit in Germany. The Heidelberg Man was named *Homo heidelbergensis*. This was followed by the Peking Man, the product of a decade of digging in a series of caves in Choukoutien in China by Canadian, Davidson Black in 1927. Here, the sample was much larger, 5 skulls, 15 smaller pieces of the skull or face, 14 lower jaws and 152 teeth. The Peking Man was named *Sinanthropus pekinensis* (China Man from Peking). The caves also contained a great many implements, some made of stone, others of the bones and antlers of animals that the cave dwellers had slaughtered. They had also presumably cooked them, because the cave floors contained layer after layer of charcoal, indicating the presence of fires that had been kept alight for long periods of time. Clearly, these cave dwellers were humans estimated to be living approximately half a million years before the present. Forty years later, anthropologist G.H.R. von Koenigswald went back to the same river in Java and found more skull pieces which tended to confirm Keith's belief that the Java Man was a man. If that was so, then the name Dubois had given it would have to be changed. Derived from the Greek word *pithecus* (ape) and *anthropus* (man), it all too clearly expressed Dubois' belief that it was indeed an evolutionary halfway step between modern apes and modern man. The implication here was that all the above fossils were manlike but not quite human enough to be called *Homo*. And yet, they certainly were not apes.

The discovery of the Peking Man provided the beginnings of a range of variations, whereas a single find like Heidelberg Man or Dubois's Java ape-man could not. Later discoveries, notably some excellent fossils from East Africa, clarified the picture to a point where all the above-mentioned fossils are now almost universally recognized as being highly variable members of a single wide-ranging species that was directly ancestral to modern man, and all of them have been given the name *Homo erectus* (erect walking man). They were *Homo*, albeit somewhat different from us. Their brains were smaller, their skulls were thicker, their eyebrow ridges more prominent and their jaws heavier. In fact, all their bones were heavier. They were exceptionally powerful, both the men and the women, with muscles to match their thick frames. It was this toughly built, medium-sized, medium-brained direct ancestor whose evolutionary escalation from *erectus* to *sapiens* is now believed to have taken place between four hundred thousand and one hundred thousand years ago (Johanson D. and Edey M., 1981:27-39).

1.1 South Africa: the first Man-apes

Dr. Raymond Dart studied a skull obtained from a young South African woman interested in fossils who had in turn brought it from the Taung lime works in 1924. The skull was of a six-year-old, with a full set of baby teeth and its six-year molars just erupting. It was definitely not a young baboon. The skull was too high and rounded, and the face was too small; baboons have long snouts and very low crowns to their heads. It appeared more like a young chimpanzee, but was too high-crowned for that. Its teeth could be neither of a chimpanzee nor a baboon. Both have large canines; in the fossil, the canines were scarcely larger than those of a human child. The foramen magnum – the hole, from which the nerves of the spinal column ascend into the brain, was at the bottom of the skull, suggesting that during its short life, this six-year-old had walked upright. In baboons and chimpanzees, the foramen magnum is located towards the back of the skull, reflecting the more nearly quadruped posture of those animals. Dart named this as *Australopithecus africanus*, the southern (*Australo*) ape (*pithecus*) from Africa. But it quickly became known as the Taung Baby, and has been so known ever since. Estimated by its finder to be as much as a million years old, this fossil was so extremely primitive that many scientists were convinced for years that it was an ape. It is, in fact, the first *Australopithecus africanus*, an authentic hominid, many of whose fossils have been found since.

Robert Broom at Strekfontein, Kromdraai in South Africa found a second type of australopithecine fossil in 1936. The fossil was like that of Taung Baby but differed in many respects. In fact, it appeared different enough to justify the creation of a new genus for it. Broom chose the name *Plesianthropus transvaalensis* (near-man from the Transvaal) for this fossil. He also found another type of fossil teeth from a schoolboy at Kromdraai, from a farm near Sterkfontein in 1938. The Kromdraai ape-man seemed more primitive than the others, not so much close as dimly foreshadowing the human condition. He settled on the name *Paranthropus* (towards man) *robustus*. The *robustus* he tagged on to underscore the specimen's larger size and generally more massive bone structure. Like Dart, Broom had no difficulty in recognizing all these South African fossils as erect-walking hominids, although he desperately needed some post-cranial bones to convince others. More fossils were found in subsequent years. The larger, robust primitive *Paranthropus* is found only in the two younger caves. The slender, more manlike little *Australopithecus/ Plesianthropus* is found only in the three older ones. Recognition of two distinct types of australopithecine in Africa came with the discovery of more fossils. The robust type has a more massive jaw and larger molars than the gracile type. It also has a prominent bony ridge on top of its skull.

Latter, Raymond Dart found another fossil at Makapansgat, north of Johannesburg, South Africa, in 1947 and named it *Australopithecus prometheus.* Broom and Robinson also found numerous fossils in the cave sites of Swarkrans, South Africa and named the species *Paranthropus crassidens.*

However, scientists have now systematized the above names, applying scientific rules for naming them. From the 1950s on, all the South African ape-men have been known as australopithecines. They are divided into two types, a slender "gracile" type and a burlier, more primitive-appearing "robust" type. The former, of which the Taung Baby was the original, the "type specimen", retained its original name of *Australopithecus africanus.* With it went all the fossils from Makapansgat and Sterkfontein; all were "gracile" types.

The big, burly specimens from Kromdraai and Swarkrans, although measurably different from the gracile species, were obviously the same general types of creature. They too were erect-walking ape-men. They were put in the same genus but into a different species. They were named *Australopithecus robustus* (Ibid: 40-70).

1.2 East Africa Man-apes and Potassium-argon Date

Louis Leakey and his wife Mary Leakey went to Olduvai, East Africa in the 1930s in search of stone tools. Olduvai lies under the rain shadow of an enormous extinct volcano, the celebrated Ngorongoro Crater. The couple had been collecting fossils from all over East Africa for years, and had managed to match certain styles in tool making with similar industries in Europe. Those at Olduvai were different. They were so primitive – single cobbles with a flake or two knocked off one end to provide a crude cutting or chopping edge, that to an untrained eye they would not have resembled shaped implements at all. Nevertheless, he and Mary recognized them for what they were, and gave the industry a name - Oldowan.

Mary found a skull popularly known as "Zinj" (means East Africa in Arabic, christened by her husband) in Olduvai in 1959. It was the first australopithecine discovered outside South Africa, and the first anywhere to be reliably dated through Potassium-argon technique of dating. Its age was 1.8 million years. It is a super-robust type, with the largest molars and jaw of any specimen found so far. No South African australopithecine has ever been found in sure association with any tool. We still don't know whether they used them. Given the lack of evidence, it looks as if they didn't. Louis, finding something special in the teeth of the fossil, named the specimen *Zinjanthropus boisei*. That name did not last long. Others, noting the close resemblance to robust types of South Africa renamed as *Australopithecus boisei*.

By the 1950s, morphological studies of Le Gros Clark had finally recognized the erect, ape-brained australopithecines, as hominids. That meant that they were members of the human family; but whether they were ancestors or cousins was could still not be determined. Most of the experts are however now willing, tentatively, to assign to *A. africanus* the place of an ancestor now, even more than before, on the basis of its presumed age.

Meanwhile, potassium-argon technique was developed by the Italian scientists to estimate the age of lava flows and volcanic ash deposits in the vicinity of Rome. This depends on measuring the amount of decay of a radioactive isotope of the element potassium into another element, argon. The 1.8 million-year date for Zinj was responsible for some astonished second looks at the dates that paleontologists had been taking down alongside their trees of mammalian evolution they have been laboriously constructing (Ibid: 71-135; Aronson, J.L. et al. 1977:323-327).

1.3 The Earliest Man – Homo habilis of East Africa

In 1962, Louis Leaky found another hominid fossil at Olduvai, East Africa. This time the fossil was not an australopithecine but a true human ancestor. In 1964 a full report was released by a team consisting of John Napier from England, Phillip Tobias (Dart's student of South Africa) and Louis himself. They had recovered some more fossils over the previous two years from this area and made a rigorous examination. These were larger-brained than australopithecine, and they placed them in the genus *Homo*. The age of this new *Homo* was estimated at 1.75 million years old and they named the fossil *Homo habilis* (handy man, a name suggested by Raymond Dart), in honour of its having been the maker of the stone tools.

However, Louis Leakey's *Homo habilis* was subjected to severe criticism for a long time. The principal reason was the scrappy condition of the evidence for the four specimens found were badly preserved. The first find, a mandible with cranial fragments, was named Johnny's Child after its finder, Leakey's son Jonathan. The second one, Cindy, was a lower jaw and teeth, some bits of an upper jaw and a patch of skull. The third, George, had only his teeth and some very small skull fragments. The fourth, Twiggy, was represented by a crushed cranium and seven teeth. Despite the fragmentary condition of these skulls, a preliminary study suggested that they were probably larger than the typical gracile skull from South Africa.

Australopithecines fell into a multimillion-year gap - between true humans and late Miocene apes. And it was Le Gros Clark's review of ape and human teeth that determined that australopithecines were not apes. But they were not humans either. Australopithecine teeth, in short, were their very own. So were their brains, which were in the 430-550 cc range, consistently larger than ape brains, notably smaller than *Homo erectus* brains (700-750 cc). That in-between condition, in brain and teeth, was what made it possible to regard australopithecines as transitional on the line of descent from apes to humans, closer to *Homo*, but not yet *Homo*.

Leakey, Napier and Tobias introduced their fossils as human and named *Homo habilis* on the basis of brain size, which was larger than the australopithecine brain. The teeth were different, more humanlike; the skull was a different shape, again more humanlike. Others criticized the suggestion because Tobias's calculation of the brain size at 642 cc was questionable because of the poor quality of the samples. They also challenged the conclusions about the teeth. They pointed out that not enough was known about the rest of *habilis*' skeleton to warrant any positive ideas about it at all. On the matter of brain size, Ralph Holloway of Columbia University, examined the specimens latter, and came up with substantially the same conclusions as Tobias. The findings of both men were later confirmed by the recovery of a nearly complete skull of a similar type in northern Kenya a few years later. Its brain was larger than any of the three in Olduvai. However, brain size alone is now recognized as a questionable index of species identification because of its variability. Thus, *Homo habilis* fell into that narrow shadow zone between *Australopithecus* and *Homo erectus*, and perhaps there was not enough room there during that time (Johanson D. and Edey M., 1981:97-104).

1.4 Omo and Clark's Biostratigraphy

The tri-national – "Cooperative International Anthropological Expedition" led by Louis Leakey carried out fossil find research at Omo. Initially, the Kenya team was lea by Leakey himself, but was soon entrusted to his son Richard Leakey. The French team was led by Arambourg but he passed away and the team was then led by a young man named Yves Coppens. The American contingent was led by Howell. Each team was set up to act independently of the others in the area specified for them. The research expedition started in 1967 and continued upto 1974.

"Geology of Omo is a marvel. It preserves a continuous record of events that is unique in the study of fossil hominid evolution. Its uniqueness results from a combination of special qualities. First it is fairly big. It is not gorge like Olduvai, but a jumble of eroded outcroppings that cover well over a hundred square miles. Second, it is deep. The deposits are more than three thousand feet thick, which means that the bottom ones is extremely old; you don't get three thousand feet of material deposited overnight. Third, it is faulted. That means that you don't have to dig down three thousand feet to get to the bottom layer. The earth's crust has tilted or buckled, and the layers are sticking up at an angle, so that even the oldest are exposed here and there on the surface of the ground. In fact, you don't have to dig at all. You just walk along. As you go, each step you take carries you forward or back in time" (Howell, F. C. 1973).

The exposed sequence of strata at Omo constituted an immense geological ruler, with sections of time marked off by about two hundred separate and distinct deposits of mud, clay, sand, gravel, and volcanic ejects. More than a hundred of these layers contained fossils. All together, they spanned about three million years in time, running roughly from four million years ago to one million years ago.

In the eight years (1967-1974) that the Omo expedition operated, it collected close to fifty thousand specimens, representing more than 140 species of mammals. Some of the little ones – rats, mice and shrews – were valuable because such small animals do not move about much and are extremely sensitive to environmental change. Equally important, Howell's practice of carefully mapping every fossil made it possible to follow the evolutionary development of various types through time. Beautiful sequences of antelopes, giraffes and elephants were obtained; new species evolving out of old ones and appearing in younger strata, then dying out as newer ones in still younger strata replaced them. Evolution, in short, was taking place before the eyes of the Omo surveyors, and they could time it! The finest examples of this process were in several lines of pigs which had been extremely common at Omo and had evolved rapidly. Basil Cooke produced family trees for pigs whose various types were so accurately dated that pigs themselves bacame measuring-sticks that could be applied to finds of questionable age in other places that had similar pigs.

This work is called biostratigraphy. What Howell did was produce a whole strip of edge with his Omo dates. The hominid finds there, although their quality was not exceptional, did fit the frame. This type of study enabled Clark Howell to review and find four different kinds. Since he knew how old they were, he could arrange them on the table, which had not been possible before, even if he could not fit them together. Equally important, some of his finds were Pliocene, more than two million years old. He had broken out of the Pleistocene, reviewed the hominids and accordingly came out as follows:

A small hominid resembling the South Africa gracile australopithecine began to appear at Omo at three million, went on certainly to 2.5 million, and might have persisted till about two million years ago, although the quality of the fossils makes that further persistence debatable.

A robust hominid, more closely resembling the super-robust Zinj than the South African *robustus* appeared at two million and disappeared at one million. Of the four types found at Omo, this one was by far the most abundant.

Traces of *Homo habilis* occurred in a few seemingly manlike teeth and are dated at about 1.85 million.

Finally, *Homo erectus*, first seen at about 1.1 million.

The review gave an idea about possible relationships hominid fossils available so far. With all the gracile types occurring before two million and all the robust ones after two million at Omo as well as in South Africa indicates that the former types might be the ancestors of the latter. Second, with *Homo habilis* occurring at Omo as well as at Olduvai after two million, speculated that it too may have had a gracile ancestor. *Homo erectus*, first seen at about 1.1 million, speculates that it too have had gracile or *habilis* ancestor (Johanson D. and Edey M., 1981:107-135).

1.5 Homo habilis of Koobi Fora

Richard Leakey started a fossil find expedition at Koobi Fora in 1969. The project was supported by the Kenyan Government. The Hominid fossils began to appear almost immediately. The team found hominids in greatest abundance were the robust australopithecines. Also found were some smaller specimens which, to Leakey, seemed to fall comfortably within the range of Cindy, George and Twiggy, those elusive *habilis* specimens from Olduvai. He hoped not only to strengthen his father's claim that *Homo habilis* existed as a valid species, but also to extend the known life of that species further back in time. The deposits were larger and richer than those at Olduvai, they went deeper into time, and many of the fossils yielded were of better quality.

In 1972, Richard Leakey announced an utterly dazzling find: a superb skull from below the KBS stuff (after the name of woman from Yale University - Kay Behrensmeyer). Inasmuch as the stuff had been dated at 2.6 million years by a pair of English potassium-argon specialists, this meant that the new skull was older than that. The new find was designated KNM-ER 1470 (Kenya National Musium – East Rudolf). The skull 1470 is Richard Leakey's most dramatic find at Koobi Fora, and one of the most important hominid fossils found anywhere. It is definitely *Homo*. The credentials of *Homo habilis* were suddenly and dramatically improved by 1470. It provided more than enough room for a species, and *Homo habilis* thereafter was generally accepted as one. It is in far better condition than any of the *habilis* specimens from Olduvai and has a larger brain. It was first thought to be nearly three million years old (2.9 million years old) – an awkward date indeed, for that made it older than many of its presumed australopithecine ancestors. More recent dating from purer ash samples has convinced most authorities that it is less than two million years old.

In fact, the only older hominids found anywhere were two from northern Kenya – an arm bone from Kanapoi that may be four million years old, and a jaw piece containing one molar from Lothagam that is about five and a half million years old. Both are too badly worn and fragmentary to reveal much about themselves, except that they are probably hominids.

There were dissenters of course. The principal one was C. Loring Brace of the University of Michigan. Brace and his followers lumped 1470 and believed in a simple family tree. It goes: *Australopithecus – Homo erectus – Homo sapiens*.

Among the most significant finds at Koobi Fora is an excellent *Homo erectus* skull. It is dated at 1.5 million years old. It lived alongside robust australopithecines and no anthropologist in the world would argue today that those two are con-specific. One of the marvels of evolution is how so many seemingly similar plants and animals have managed to find ways of making a living cheek by jowl with each other. This seems to have been the case for early hominids as well. The gracile/ Homo type begins to emerge as a smaller-jawed, smaller-toothed omnivore; the robust type as an increasingly specialized eater of coarse vegetable matter. That divergence in diet alone would be enough to permit the coexistence of two types of erect hominids. Thanks to Richard Leakey, through his findings we know today that two did coexist (Ibid:136-149).

1.6 The Hadar Hominids

The Hadar, Ethopia expedition camp was established on a low bluff overlooking the Awash River in 1973. The first expedition team led by Johanson concentrated mostly on geology and surveying, and was notably thin on paleontological expertise. Their first hominid find at Hadar was a knee joint, dated as more than three million years old, the oldest such fossil on record. The angle at which the two bones connect is what convinced paleoanthropologists that it was a hominid. In apes. the connection would be straight. The hominid knee joints are oval; those of the ape are round. A manlike knee joint meant manlike walking. This would be the first evidence from anywhere that anything had walked upright three million years ago.

The second expedition was held in 1974. The Johanson and Taib's team this time consisted of Basil Cooke, the pig specialist; Michel Beden, the elephant specialist; Vera Eisenmann, the horse specialist; Germaine Petter, the carnivores specialist; Jean-Jacques Jaeger, the rodent specialist; and Claude Guerin, the rhinoceros specialist. Alemayehu Asfaw, a good fossil finder was in the team and found a hominid jaw, then another upper jaw with every one of its teeth in position. Tigrean, another worker of the team found the third jaw. In australopithecines, the molars are very large and the incisors, the front teeth are very small. In humans the reverse is true. Our molars are small, and our incisors comparatively large. The jaws collected were more human than australopithecine. The canines, on the other hand, seemed neither human nor australopithecine and held a hint of a more apelike condition. Their peculiar blend of Homo and australopithecine traits, with a whiff of something more primitive, was utterly baffling. Adding to the perplexity was a size problem: although both of Alemayehu's specimens were adults, one was much larger than the other, suggesting the coexistence of two species of hominids at Hadar. Another significant find at Hadar was the *Hipparion* horse's teeth with intact ectostylid that became extinct some time after three million B.C. The true horse *Equus* is a migrant from Asia and appears in East Africa at two million (Ibid:176-177).

The most significant find of Hadar was of Lucy by Gray and Johanson. Lucy was utterly mind-boggling; there was no other way to describe her. At nearly half of a complete skeleton (40%), Lucy seemed incredible to the scientists even as they saw the evidence accumulating before their eyes. It was not more than three and a half feet tall, had a tiny brain, and yet walked erect. Its jaw was V-shaped, not as rounded in front as some of the other mandibles, and smaller than any of them. Furthermore, its first premolar had only a single cusp. The larger jaws had two-cusped premolars. Since the one cusp condition is the more primitive and the two-cusp condition the more human, experts concluded that Lucy was different from the larger-jawed type. Lucy proved that hominids had walked erect at three million B.C. More surprising yet, they had walked before their brains had begun to enlarge (Ibid:164-185).

During the third Hadar Field Season in 1975, the Johanson's team found the First Family at site 333. The fossils were: one was a hominid heel bone, other was a femur, teeth at the bottom of the slope and two other bones halfway up, two fibulas, two shin bones; indicating the presence of more than one individual (Ibid: 208-219).

Dating the Hadar fossils took seven years and required the synchronization of five techniques: geology, potassium-argon dating, fission-track dating, paleomagnetism, and biostratigraphy. All were necessary for the gradual development of a detailed and accurate stratigraphic column. Aronson, an expert on potassium-argon dating is now reasonably sure that the basalt is 3.75 million years old. That would make Lucy and the first Family close to 3.5 million years old, the jaws and knee joint close to 4.0 million years old (Ibid:187-207).

1.7 Lucy and Laetoli Hominids

Hominid fossils inclusive of Lucy of Hadar and the hominid fossils and footprints of Laetoli reveal that around three million years ago, erect walking hominid evolution took place in Hadar and Laetoli. *Homo* traits in fossils of that age could be seen in these fossils. The teeth of the fossils had already evolved away from an ape condition and were clearly more human. In the fossils, premolars and molars are smaller and the front teeth larger and these are human traits. But they also had traits that made them different from human teeth. They had very big back teeth, some of them were truly massive, twice the size of a modern human molar. Secondly, the enamel on the back teeth was extremely thick, much thicker than in human teeth. Thirdly, the front teeth were remarkably smaller in comparison with the back teeth. The ones with massive jaws and molars were Australopithecines, while the ones with smaller jaws and molars were *Homo*. Biometric analysis demonstrated that the Hadar and

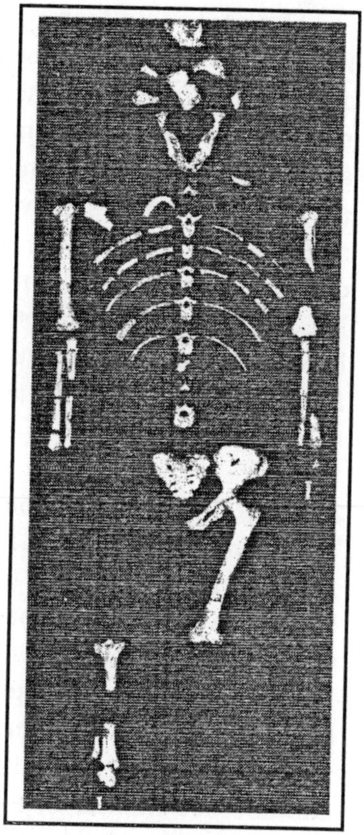

Lucy (fossil)

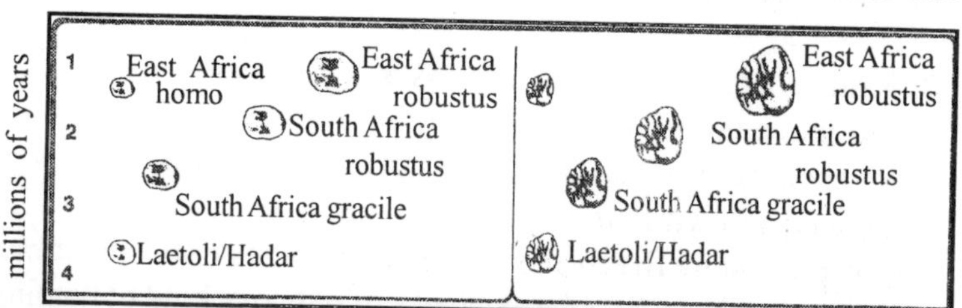

Teeth Arrangement: premolar (left) molar (right) of Human Ancestors.

Laetoli hominids were not Homo but some kind of early australopithecine (Ibid: 255-278).

The analysis which positions teeth from left to right in increasing order of size, and from top to bottom according to age, makes clear that "small" was "primitive", and that large molar size never occured in humans, but appeared later among australopithecines, reaching its maximum in the younger robust types. The examples shown in the chart are premolars (left) and molars (right). It was the australopithecine teeth that had changed. They had gone in a direction of their own to satisfy a life-style somewhat different from that being lived by early humans, a life-style that would become increasingly specialized for coarse vegetarian diet and lead to the development of larger and larger teeth (ibid: 255-278).

1.8 Laetoli fossils and footprints

Between 1974 and 1977 Mary Leakey and her team found forty-two hominid teeth, some of them, associated with bits of jawbone. One in particular LH-4 (Laetoli Hominid 4), was a fine specimen, a mandible with nine teeth in place. They also found some hominid footprints, one of the most extraordinary cases of preservation and discovery in all of paleoanthropology. The hominid footprints of one adult man and another smaller of a pregnant woman walking together were found just below the present surface of the ground in some shallow layers of ash and were extremely fragile. The hominid fossils and footprints of Laetoli were dated three million years old (ibid: 236-252).

2. Family Tree of Human Ancestors

In paleoanthropology, before the discovery of fossils and Lucy at Hadar and fossils and footprints at Laetoli, there were three well-known Family trees of human ancestors. The First one, espoused by Brace and others, recognizes only one branch of the hominid tree, and the existence of only one kind of hominid at a time. Recently, however, Brace has permitted the branching off of *Australopithecus robustus*, because it is too unlike the *Homo* types that follow it to fit on the man line. The virtue of this tree is its simplicity. Brace, a "lumper" does not accept *Homo habilis* as a valid species. He lumps it with *Australopithecus africanus* (tree at left).

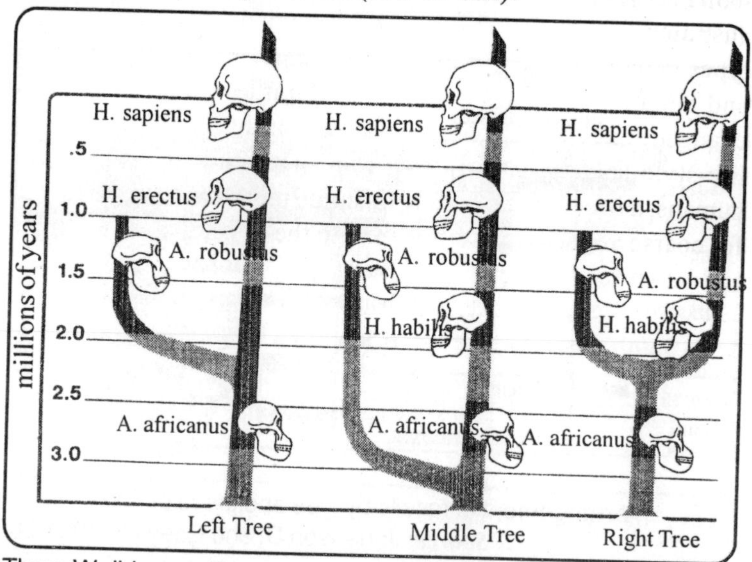

Three Well-known Family Trees of 1960s-70s
Source: Johanson D. and Edey M., 1981:281

The second family tree, reflecting the views of John Robinson, attempts to restore the awkward contradiction, which results from the observation that "robust" types have more "primitive back teeth than gracile" types, although, on the evidence of South African caves, they are younger. Robinson's solution was to place the "robust" types correctly in time (2.0 to 1.0 million years ago) and then assume a common ancestor with the "gracile" *Australopithecus africanus* (centre tree).

The third family tree, the most accepted in the 1960s and 1970s, reflects a growing consensus that *A. africanus* was ancestral to both *A. robustus* and *Homo habilis*. It acknowledges that increased molarization of the teeth through time was an australopithecine trait, not a human one, but assumes that this tendency, already evident in *A. africanus*, was not evidence enough to dislodge it as a human ancestor (right Family tree).

Realizing that none of these family trees could accommodate the new evidence produced by Johanson and White from their fossil studies at Hadar and Laetoli, they decided to draw a new tree of their own.

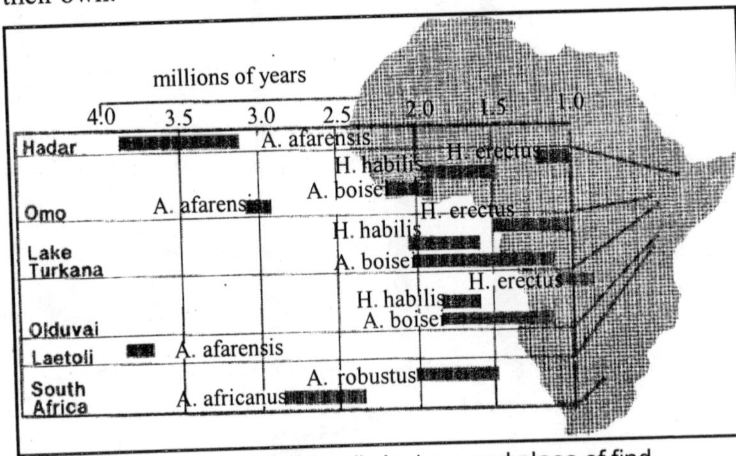

Arrangement of fossils by type and place of find

Source: Johanson D. and Edey M., 1981:283

They placed all the African hominids on a diagram according to their age, type and location. To place the South African fossils, they used the most recent estimates of Elizabeth Vaba, a South African biostratigrapher, for the ages of both the "robust" and the "gracile" types. For Omo, they already had good dates. For Lake Turkana, they took Curtis' potassium-argon dates and the fossil pig evidence and accepted Richard Leakey's identification of the fossils there. For Olduvai, Hadar and Laetoli they took the published potassium-argon dates. The next step was to simplify by ignoring locality and pulling the fossils together by type (ibid: 283).

Consolidating the information in the chart above, the simplest family tree of the human ancestors has been derived. All the *A. afarensis* fossils can be lumped between 4.0 and 3.0 million, all the *A. africanus* ones between 2.7 and 2.2 million, all the *A. robustus* between 2.1 and 1.0, and so on. They are convinced that *A.*

afarensis, the oldest and most primitive hominid known, was ancestral to all others. They reason that increased molarization was a late australopithecine phenomenon and they have located the types that display it accordingly, with *A. robustus*, the most heavily molarized, at the end of that line. That leaves the *Homo* types, with back teeth essentially unchanged from those of their ancestor *A. afarensis*, on a line of their own, with the increasingly advanced *Homo erectus* and *Homo sapiens* evolving out of *Homo habilis*. Tools, as the chart indicates, are a *Homo*, not an australopithecine, invention (Ibid: 284-287).

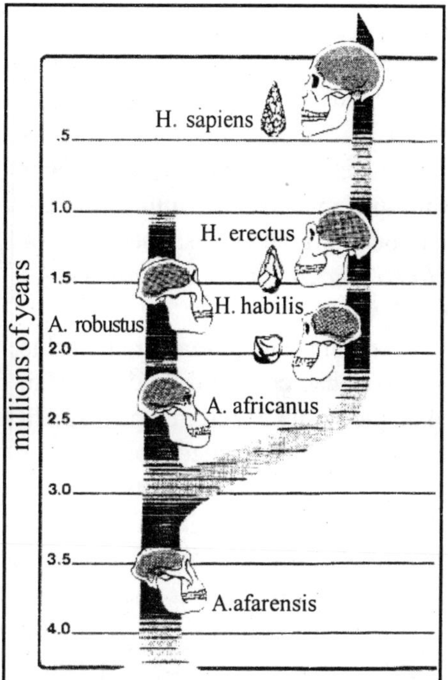

Family Tree of Human Ancestors
Source: Johanson D. and Edey M., 1981:284

In 1856, J.C. Fuhlrott a German science teacher dug out a fossil from a quarry near his home as displayed them as bones of a man, but not those of a modern man. This was the first non-modern human fossil ever found and named the Neanderthal Man evolved from *Homo erectus,* estimated between 200,000 to 75,000 years ago with larger brain and eye ridges. It underwent decades of controversy. Some think it was the same species as us. Others think it was an ancestor. There are a few who consider it a kind of cousin. That matter is unresolved because many of the best Neanderthal fossils were collected in Europe before anybody knew how to excavate sites properly or conduct proper dating. Consequently, we do not have exact age for most of the Neanderthal fossils.

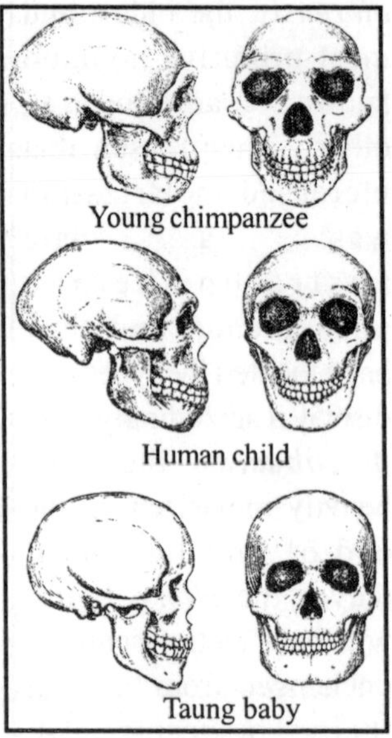

One and a half million years of evolution in humans has produced a higher and rounder skull, a much larger brain, and a distinct chin (which is missing in *Homo erectus*), the modern thinking man *Homo sapiens*. There has been a gradual disappearance of *Homo erectus'* heavy eyebrow ridges (Ibid: 43).

An amateur scientist, Charles Dawson, had collected Piltdown Man skull pieces in 1912 from a gravel pit in England. It was named *Eoanthropus dawsoni*. No date could be ascertained in this case either. It had a very large brain, comparable to that of a modern man. Instead of a human jaw, it had one shaped like that of an ape; in fact, it could have been an ape jaw except that it had manlike molars, flat on their grinding surface (Ibid: 49).

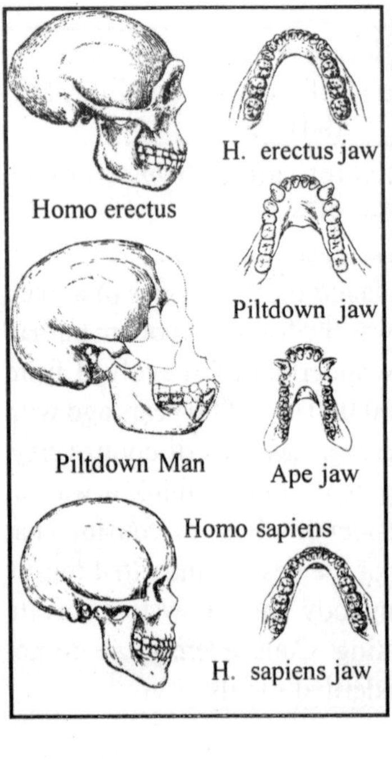

The problem with the Piltdown Man becomes clear when it is compared with *Homo erectus* and modern *Homo sapiens*. The Piltdown cranium is like that of modern man in shape and size and not like *Homo erectus* at all. But its jaw is more primitive than either, having the boxlike configuration and huge pointed canine of large apes. It appears to be made up of a human skull and an ape jaw arbitrarily joined together, which is what it ultimately turned out to be.

Cro-Magnon Man, so named for the locality in Southern France was found where the bones were first unearthed. Many specimens were recovered; among them were complete skeletons so virtually indistinguishable from those of present humans that even the most skeptical had to concede that they were human. Cro-Magnon Man had been living there for forty or fifty thousand years and may have disappeared as recently as ten thousand years ago. They were men like us, men who could paint beautiful pictures and could presumably think complex thoughts, men who routinely made a variety of useful stone tools and clearly had an elaborate culture, in many respects, more sophisticated than some of the so-called "savage" cultures found in isolated parts of the earth to this day.

Homo sapiens sapiens, the modern man, evolved from the older *Homo erectus* fifty thousand years ago (Ibid:281-293).

3. The Spread of humans around the world

The human history of origin remained confined to Africa for about 3.0 to 4.0 million years ago. The first human ancestor to spread beyond Africa was the excellent hunter-gatherer *Homo erectus*, as is attested by fossils discovered on the Southeast Asia

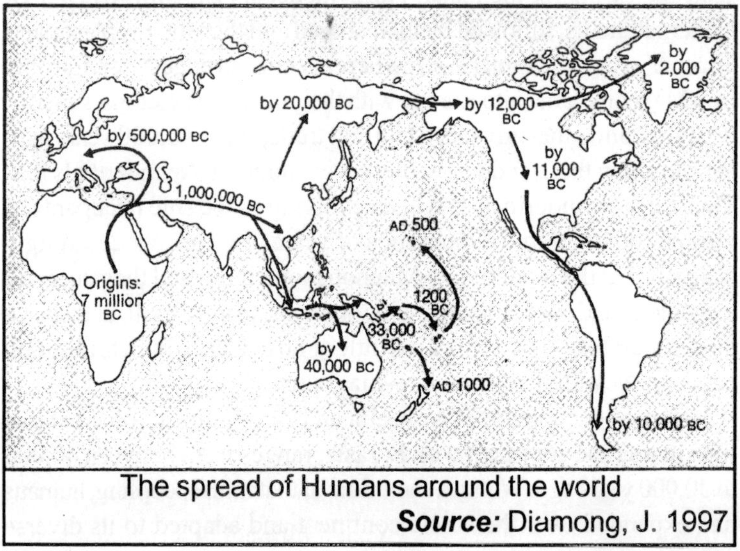

The spread of Humans around the world

Source: Diamong, J. 1997

island of Java and known as the Java Man; and second in Choukoutien, China, known as Peking Man dated to a million years ago. The earliest unquestioned evidence for humans in Europe stems from around half a million years ago from Neanderthals. One would certainly assume that the colonization of Asia also permitted the simultaneous colonization of Europe, since Eurasia is a single landmass not bisected by major barriers. But evidence from half a million years ago suggests that human fossils had diverged from older *Homo erectus* skeletons in their enlarged, rounder, and less angular skulls. African and European skulls of half a million years ago were sufficiently similar to human skulls, so modern that they are classified in our species, *Homo sapiens*, instead of in *Homo erectus*. This distinction is due to evolution from *Homo erectus* to *Homo sapiens*. About half a million years ago, human populations of Africa and western Eurasia started to diverge from each other and from East Asian populations in skeletal details. Many skeletons known as Neanderthals and sometimes classified as a separate species, *Homo neanderthalensis*, represent the population of Europe and Western Asia between 130,000 and 40,000 years ago. Neanderthals were the first humans to leave behind strong evidence of burying their dead and caring for their sick. The evidence for a localized origin of modern humans, followed by their spread and then their replacement of other types of humans elsewhere, seems strongest for Europe. Cro-Magnons came into Europe with their modern skeletons, superior weapons, and other advanced cultural traits, some 40,000 years ago. Within a few thousand years, there were no more Neanderthals left. This, after Neanderthals had been evolving as the sole occupants of Europe for hundreds of thousands of years. That sequence strongly suggests that the modern Cro-Magnons somehow used their superior technology and their language skills or brains, to infect, kill, or displace the Neanderthals, leaving behind little or no evidence of hybridization between Neanderthals and Cro-Magnons.

Human occupation of Australia and New Guinea, joined at that time in a single continent with Eurasia, ranges from between 40,000 to 30,000 years ago. Within a short time of that initial peopling, humans had expanded over the whole continent and adapted to its diverse habitats - from the tropical rain forests and high mountains of New Guinea to the dry interior and wet southeastern corner of Australia.

During the Ice Ages, so much of the oceans' water was locked up in glaciers that sea levels dropped hundreds of feet below Asia and the Indonesian islands of Sumatra, Borneo, Java, and Bali became dry lands. As did other shallow straits, such as the Bering Strait and the English Channel. Thus, humans occupied these islands about 33,000 years ago, probably by paddling across. Another extension of human range that soon followed was the one into the coldest parts of Eurasia – to Siberia by 20,000 years ago.

It is uncertain when, but it is speculated that the Americas were first colonized around 14,000 years ago. The oldest unquestioned human remains in the Americas are at sites in Alaska dated to around 12,000 B.C., followed by a population of sites in the United States south of the Canadian border and in Mexico in the centuries just before 11,000 B.C. The latter sites are called Clovis sites, named after the type-site near the town of Clovis, New Mexico, where their characteristic large stone spear points were first recognized. Clovis descendants would reach Patagonia, lying 8,000 miles south of the United States, Canada border, in less than a thousand years. The Siberians crossed to Alaska, either by sea across the Bering Strait or on foot at glacial times when the Bering Strait was dry land. The Bering land bridge, during its millennia of intermittent existence, would have been upto a thousand miles wide, covered by open tundra, and easily traversable by people adapted to cold conditions. The bridge was flooded and became a strait again fairly recently when sea level rose around 14,000 B.C.

Soon thereafter, a north-south ice-free corridor opened in the Canadian ice sheet, permitting the first Alaskans to pass through and come out in the Great Plains around the site of the modern Canadian city of Edmonton. That removed the last serious barrier between Alaska and Patagonia for modern humans. The Edmonton pioneers would have found the Great Plains tempting, teaming as they were with game and they were the excellent hunter-gatherers. They would have thrived, increased in numbers, and gradually spread south to occupy the whole hemisphere. The Americas could thus have first been settled around 11,000 B.C., and quickly filled up with people reaching southern end of South America by 10,000 B.C.

The settlement of the world's remaining islands was not completed until modern times. Mediterranean islands such as Crete, Cyprus, Corsica, and Sardinia were inhabited between about 8,500 and 4,000 B.C. Caribbean islands were inhabited around 4,000 B.C. Polynesian and Micronesian islands peopled in between 1,200 B.C. and 1,000 A.D. Madagascar was inhabited by humans sometimes between 300 and 800 A.D. And Iceland was inhabited only in the Ninth century A.D. Native Americans, possibly ancestral to the modern Inuit, spread throughout the High Artic around 2,000 B.C. That left, as the sole uninhabited areas awaiting European explorers over the last 700 years, only the most remote islands of the Atlantic and Indian Oceans such as the Azores and Seychelles, plus Antarctica (Diamond, J.1997 :35-52).

4. When did our Ancestors start walking upright?

Our hominid ancestors learned to walk upright in the forest, not out on the Savanna, even though that's where they were found living later. When they arrived in the Savanna, they were already bipeds. Fossil evidence reveals that they learned to walk upright between 3.0 and 4.0 million years ago. And they did it without the benefit of tools. The reason of upright walking was primarily sexual and social.

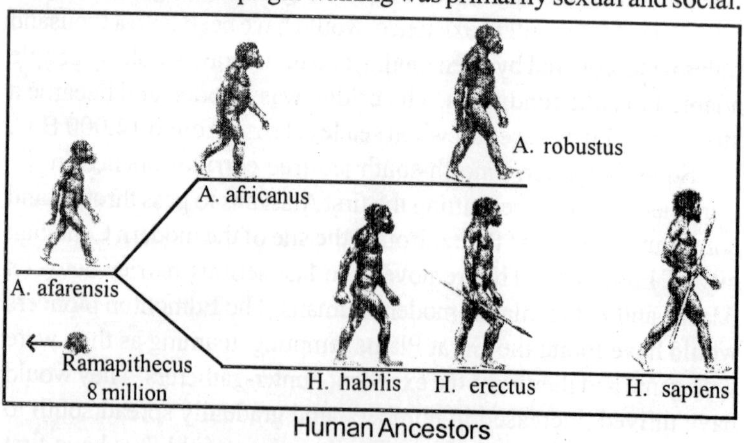

Human Ancestors

Source: Johanson D. and Edey M., 1981:286-87

Once they had perfected upright walking, they were free to walk wherever they chose, because upright walking itself is not inefficient. Upright walkers can walk all day as well as quadrants and it's only when they try to run that the quadrants are faster than bipeds. The fossil finds of Hadar, such as the knee joint, the first family, the jaws, Lucy, and fossils and footprints of Laetoli, lumped and named as *Australopithcus afarensis* are evidences of upright walking dated between 3.0 and 4.0 million years old. Tool using was insignificant around 3.0-4.0 million years ago. *Homo habilis* started using tools only in 2.5 million years ago. Our hominid ancestors were socially and sexually innovative apes who became bipeds and, as a result, managed to propagate human kind better than other apes. It was sheer luck that the human ability to stand up, leaving his hands free that led to a latter development of tools and a culture, and a still larger brain in modern humans (Lovejoy, C.O., 1980:52-250).

5. When did our Ancestors start using tools?

Calculating the age of a stone tools is not easy. Stone does not lend itself to radiometric dating even though it may have been made of volcanic rock. The reason is that the hominid that made it, may have picked up a piece that was fifty or a hundred million years older than he was.

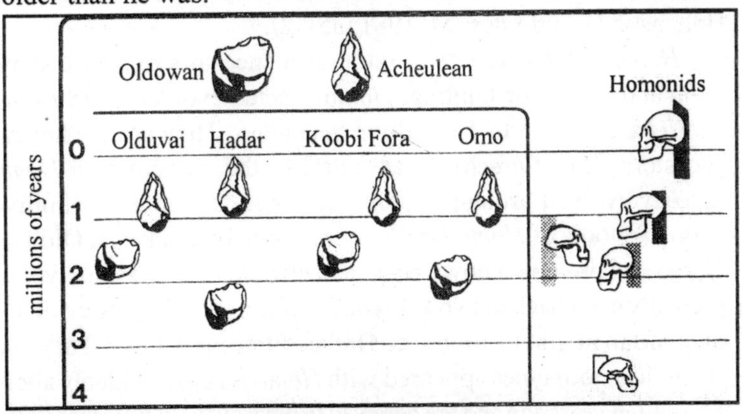

Types of Stone Tools

Source: Johanson D. and Edey, M. 1981: 231

He may even have made the tool in one place and dropped it in another. Thus, stone tools have played a mixed role in the elucidation of early African prehistory.

The Hadar-Laetoli fossil specimens (*Australopithecus afarensis*) represent a common ancestor to the later australopithecines (*Australopithecus africanus* and *Australopithecus robustus*) and to *Homo* (*Homo habilis, Homo erectus,* and *Homo sapiens*). Divergence between the latter two types probably began around three million years ago. One line of evolution leading to australopithecines the *Australopithecus africanus* represents an intermediate stage on the way to *Australopithecus robustus* evolved from the ancestor *Australopithecus afarensis*. Paleoanthropologists however do not believe that this line was ancestral to humans. They believe that the humans evolved from another branch of *Australopithecus afarensis*, a process which began some three million years ago and was accomplished about two million years ago. By then, the human ancestors recognizable as *Homo habilis* walked on earth. So did other cousins, the *Australopithecus africanus* and *Australopithecus robustus*. For about a million years they appear to have lived side by side. A million years back, there were no australopithecines left. They had become extinct. There is no fossil evidence to prove that the australopithecines were using tools (Johanson D. and Edey, M. 1981: 35-52*)*.

Homo habilis were the first human ancestors to devise stone tools and use it for hunting. *Homo erectus* evolved from *Homo habilis* around 1.5 to 1.0 million years ago. They are the human ancestors. *Homo erectus* is ancestral to the modern man *Homo sapiens* evolved around 50,000 years ago. Extremely primitive Oldowan tools of *Homo habilis* were found by Leakey at Olduvai Gorge and are now known to date back at least 1.8 million years, probably even back to two and a half million years, on the evidence of similar artifacts found at Hadar, Omo and Lake Turkana. Acheulean tool types appeared with *Homo erectus* suddenly about 1.5 million years ago and are believed to have evolved little thereafter. Both *Homo erectus* and Acheulean tool types were stubbornly resistant to change for at least a million years. It would seem that the needs of an Early African hunter-gatherer were adequately served by the Acheulean toolkit and that there was little or no reason to improve it further. An arrangement of Oldown and Acheulean tools according to site and age reveals that the Oldowan are probably the work of *Homo habilis* and that the Acheulean are the work of *Homo erectus*. Oldowan tools at 2.5 million from Hadar suggest that *Homo habilis* may ultimately turn out to be that old also, since there is no good evidence from anywhere to indicate that australopithecines made tools of either type. Apparently stone tools are an invention of *Homo* (Ibid: 278-293).

6. Food Habits of the Human ancestor and its impact on Larger Animals

The earliest known human ancestors of 8.0 to 10.0 million years ago such as *Ramapithecus, Sivapithecus, Gigantopithecus, Limnopithecus, Hispanopithecus, Ouranopithecus* and *Rudapithecus* lived on essentially vegetarian diet, and perhaps occasionally catching small prey. This condition of vegetarian diet of our ancestors probably remained more or less unchanged upto around 3.0 million years ago (until the disappearance of *Australopithecus afarensis*). With the bifurcation of evolutionary lines into the populations of Australopithecine and *Homo* sometime around three million years ago, divergence in the food habits of our ancestors becomes evident. The australopithecines (*A. africanus* and *A. robustus*) fed on more and more coarse vegetarian diet with the development of larger mandible, larger premolars and molars. On the *Homo* line (human ancestors *Homo habilis, Homo erectus*) the molars remained unchanged. But with their invention of Oldowan stone tools by *Homo habilis* and Acheulean tools by *Homo erectus*, their food habits specialized to an omnivorous diet. They developed better hunting skills with their newly invented stone tools and became excellent hunter-gathers. They could live on any kind of diet depending on availability and this is one of the main reasons of their survival.

Homo erectus evolved into *Homo sapiens* and finally into a very successful hunter-gatherer. Their diet consisted of fruits, vegetables, roots and tubers, tender shoots, scavenging and hunting of both small and large animals (Ibid:278-293).

7. Extermination of large animal species by humans

With the spread of *Homo spp. (H. habilis, H. erectus, H. sapiens),* rapid extermination of large animal species took place. Eurasia, the world's largest continent was the first victim of mass extermination of large animal species by humans. Today, we regard Africa as the continent of big mammals. Africa was the least affected continent in the extermination binge launched by humans. In spite of Africa's long occupation before the colonization of Eurasia a million years ago, the proto-humans were at such a primitive stage then that they posed no serious threat to the larger animals there. Though not in the manifest abundance of Africa's Serengeti Plains, Modern Eurasia also had many species of big mammals such as Asia's rhinos, elephants and tigers, and Europe's moose and bears and until classical times lions. Most big mammals of Africa and Eurasia survived into modern times because they had coevolved with proto-humans for hundreds of thousands or even millions of years. They therefore received ample time to evolve a fear of humans as our ancestors' hunting skills improved. In contrast to Africa and then Eurasia, Australia/ New Guinea today has no equally large mammals, in fact no mammal larger than the 100 lbs. kangaroos. This continent formerly had its own suite of diverse big mammals, including giant kangaroos, rhino-like marsupial leopards. It also had a 400 lbs. ostrich-like flightless bird, impressively big reptiles including a one-tone lizard, a giant python and land-dwelling crocodiles. This mega-fauna of Australia/ New Guinea disappeared with the arrival of humans around 40,000 B.C. These big animals had the misfortune suddenly being confronted, without any evolutionary preparation; by invading modern humans possessing fully developed hunting skills. The invading humans hunted these big animals indiscriminately for food, pushing them into extinction. Similarly, the dodo of Mauritious, giant lemurs of Madagascar, the big flightless geese of Hawaii etc are examples of extermination by humans. Soon after the arrival of humans in Siberia around 20,000 B.C. Eurasia's wooly mammoth and wooly rhinoceros went extinct.

Like Australia, the Americas had originally been full of big mammals. About 15,000 years ago, the American West looked much as Africa's Serengeti Plains do today, with herds of elephants and horses pursued by lions and cheetahs, and joined by members of such exotic species as camels and giant ground sloth. Just as in Australia/ New Guinea, so in the Americas, most of those large mammals were hunted to extinction. While the extinctions probably took place 30,000 years ago in Australia, they occurred around 12,000 years back in the America. For those extinct American mammals whose bones are available in greatest abundance and have been dated especially accurately, one can pinpoint the extinctions as having occurred around 11,000 B.C. Perhaps the most accurately dated extinctions are those of the Shasta ground sloth and Harrington's mountain goat in the Grand Canyon area; both disappeared within a century or two of 11,000 B.C. The hunters expanding southward through the Americas, encountering big animals that had never seen humans before would have found American animals easy kills and ended up exterminating them.

The spread of human habitation having excellent hunting-gathering skills and omnivorous diets around the world has been mainly responsible for extermination of larger animals from many newly inhabited continents and island of the world. Added to this is the climate change factor often reasoned for extinction of many big animal species. Extensive extermination of big animals by human hunter-gatherers, and excessive extraction of wild food-plants continued upto the end of 12,000 B.C. The age also marks the end of the Pleistocene Era and the last of Ice Age. The end of Pleistocene Era marks the scarcity of food for the hunter-gatherers due to excessive killing of bigger animals and also excessive harvest of wild food-plants the world over, which compelled the human race to find alternative means of food for survival in some parts of the world. The situation also compelled the human race to think over domestication of plants and animals for food, give up their nomadic lifestyles and start village or settled life with agriculture at least in some parts of the world for survival. However, many isolated countries or places inhabited by primitive tribes continue a hunting-gathering lifestyle even today (Diamond, J. 1997: 157-175).

8. Human habitation in Sikkim

Archeologists organize the chronology of human habitation into several periods.

(i) Archaic Period (c. 38,000 B.C. - 2,500 B.C): migration of human beings which started about 40,000 years ago from Africa.

(ii) Formative or Pre-classic Period (c. 2,500 - 100 B.C.): Village grew in size and population.

(iii) Proto-classic Period (c. 100 B.C. -300 A.D.): Complex Urban cultures began.

(iv) Classic Period (c. A.D.300 - 900): writing reached a high level of complexicity; peak of the classic culture.

(v) Post-classic Period (c. A.D. 900 - 1520): abandonment of classic cultures and beginning of modern cities.

So far as habitation of Sikkim is concerned, the aboriginal Lepcha and Limboo mythology (oral myths) maintains that Greater Sikkim was inhabited by these aboriginal tribes from the Archaic period of human migration (c. 38,000 - 2,500 B.C.). The Limboo Mundhum (oral myth) describes that the Limboo progenitors were created by their creator god *Sigera Yabhundin Mang Porokmi Wambhami Mang* with the blessing of the Almighty Goddess *Tagera Ningwaphuma* at Phoktanglungma-Pembenlungma (Kumbhakarna/Jannu) mountain through the process of biogenesis. Similarly, the Lepcha tradition narrates that the Lepcha progenitors were created by their Goddess *Itbu-mo* out of the untroden snow of Kangchenjunga at the mountain itself (Subba, J.R. 1999; 2005; 2008).

Historical evidence of the human habitation in this part of the Himalayan region is available only from the Pre-classic or Formative period (c. 2,500 - 100 B.C.) onwards. Legend has it that there were 29 Rajas/ Kings of the Kirant (Limboo, Khambu, Yakha) Dynasty of Nepal beginning with Yalamber, whose capital in the beginning was at Yalung, on the bank of Yalung River, a tributory of Tamber River in Limbuan - the land of the Limboo tribes, now in Eastern Nepal. Limbuan is the landmass bounded by the Arun River to the West and Mechi River in the East and was a part of Greater Sikkim between 1642 A.D. to 1733 A.D. During the reign of the seventh Kirant King, Jitedasti, Sakya Simha (Buddha) is believed to have come to Nepal. The Kiranti oral history also hands down that Jitedasti assisted the Pandavas in the great war of Mahabharara and was killed in battle which dates back to about 600 B.C. During the reign of Stunko (226 B.C.), the fourteenth king of this dynasty, Ashoka, the king of Pataliputra (Patna), came to Nepal (Vansittart, E. 1896:10-27).

Similarly, the first Lepcha king (Panu), Thekong Adek ruled the present area of Sikkim in the 7th century A.D. (Classic Period). Subsequently, 10 Lepcha Kings/ Panus (the religious and administrative tribal chiefs) ruled this part of Sikkim upto 1642 A.D (Classic and Postclassic period). The last Panu was Thekong Mon Solong who continued his kingship till the establishment or formation of a Chiefdom with Namgyal Dynasty in Greater Sikkim (Halfdan, Siegen 1967; Subba, J.R. 2008:2-3).

Greater Sikkim (inclusive of Limbuwan in present day Nepal, Chumbi valley now in Tibet, and Har Chu and Ammo Chu valleys in present day Bhutan) was inhabited mainly by Lepcha, Limboo and Bhutia tribes, the last arriving after the 13th century A.D. They continued their hunting-gathering lifestyles till the end of eighteenth century (1890 A.D.). They were still primarily hunter-gatherers also practising shifting cultivation (slash and burn cultivation) on the sloppy mountainous lands.

This is evident from the "Himalayan Journal - Notes of Naturalist" by Hooker J.D Vol. I: pp123-124 who visited Sikkim on November 1949. In his own words:

> ".. rice forming their chief sustenance; ..grown without irrigation, and produced a large, flat, coarse grain which becomes gelatinous, and often pink, when cooked. Pork is a staple dish, and they also eat elephant, and all kinds of animal food. When traveling, they live on whatever they can find, whether animal or vegetable. Fern-tops, roots of Scitamincce, and other flower-buds, various leaves, and fungi are chopped up, fried, and eaten. They drink out of little wooden cups, turned from knots of maple or other wood. ... Their intoxicating drink, which seems more to excite them to debauch the mind, is partially fermented Murwa grain (*Eleusine coracana*) finger millet. Spirits are rather too strong to be relished raw, and when a glass of wine is given to one of the party he sips it, and hands it round to all the rest. ... They never inhabit the same spot for more than three successive years, after which the Rajah demands an increased rent. They therefore, squat in any place, which he can render profitable for that period, and then moves to another. His first operation, after selecting a site is to burn the jungle; then he clears away the trees, and cultivates between the stumps. Some low steep spurs were well cultivated, though the angle of the field was upwards of 25 degree, the crops, chiefly maize. Large fish, chiefly Cyprinoid, were abundant in the beautifully clear water of the rivers."

Only in the last decade of the nineteenth century (1890s A.D.), when the Colonial British Administration started settling Nepalese from Nepal by clearing the forest, did settled agriculture on permanent basis through bench terracing of the lands for cultivation begin in Sikkim.

2
Food Production

The end of the Pleistocene Era and the last Ice Age corresponds approximately to 11,000 B.C. which, marks the beginning of village life evolving in a few parts of the world. Geologists term it the start of Recent Era. Within a thousand years of this date, humans also started plant and animal domestication in at least some parts of the world. Ever since the ancestors of modern humans diverged from the ancestors of the apes, as described in the previous chapter, all humans on earth fed themselves exclusively by hunting wild animals and gathering wild plants. It was only in the last 11,000 years that humans turned to what is termed producing their own food by domesticating wild animals and plants and eating the resulting livestock and crops. Today, most humans consume food that they produce themselves or someone else produces for them. At current rates of change, within the next few decades, the few remaining bands of hunter-gatherers will abandon their ways, disintegrate, or die out, thereby ending millions of years of commitment to the hunter-gatherer lifestyle.

Different people acquired food production skills at different times in prehistory. Some aboriginal tribes never acquired it at all. Of those who did, some developed it independently , while others acquired it from neighbours. Availability of more consumable calories means more people. Among wild plants and animal species, only a small portion are edible or worth hunting or gathering. Most species are useless to us as food, for one or more of the following reasons: they are indigestible, poisonous, low in nutritional value, tedious to prepare, difficult to gather, or dangerous to hunt. Most biomass of land is in the form of wood and leaves, most of which we cannot digest. However, by selecting and growing the few species of plants and animals that we can eat, we obtain far more edible calories per acre. Similarly, by domesticating selected animals we obtain meat, milk, manure for crops, and power to pull ploughs for cultivation. With time, domestic animals became a major source of protein, replacing wild game.

1. Independent Centres of Wild Plants and Animals Domestication of the World:

As mentioned earlier, in a few places food production developed independently. In most other places, it was imported in the form of crops and livestock that had been domesticated elsewhere. There are only five areas in the world for which the evidence that they developed food production independently is at present detailed and compelling. These are:

(i) Southwest Asia, also known as the Near East or the Fertile Crescent;
(ii) China;
(iii) Mesoamerica – the term applied to central and southern Mexico and adjacent areas of Central America;
(iv) The Andes of South America, and possibly the adjacent Amazon Basin as well; and
(v) The Eastern United States.

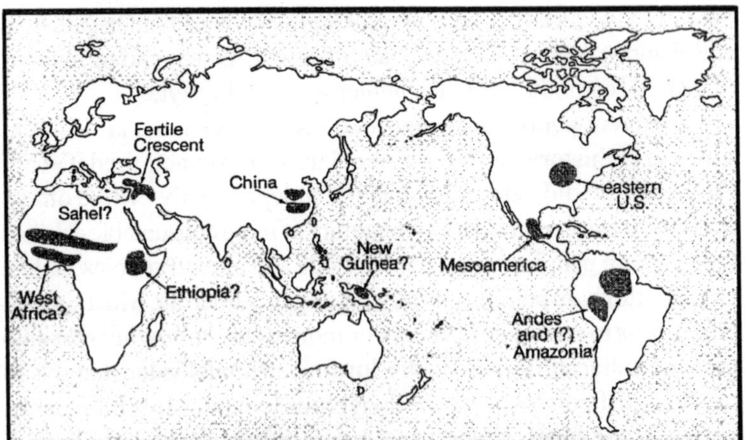

Centers of origin of food production

Source: Diamond J. 1997

Some or all of these centers may actually comprise several nearby centers where food production arose more or less independently such as North China's Yellow River valley and South China's Yangtse River valley.

In addition to these four areas where food production definitely arose de novo, five others:

(vi) Africa's Sahel Zone,

(vii) Tropical West Africa,

(viii) Ethiopia, and

(ix) New Guinea, are candidates for their distinction.

There is, however, some uncertainty in each case. Although indigenous wild plants were undoubtedly domesticated in Africa's Sahel zone just south of the Sahara, cattle herding may have preceded agriculture there and it is not yet certain whether these were independently domesticated Sahel cattle or, instead, domesticated cattle of Fertile Crecent origin whose arrival triggered local plant domestication. It remains similarly uncertain whether the arrival of Sahel crops then triggered the undoubted local domestication of indigenous wild plants in tropical West Africa, and whether the arrival of Southwest Asian crops is what triggered the local domestication of indigenous wild plants in Ethiopia. As for New Guinea, archaeological studies there have provided evidence of early agriculture well before food production in any adjacent area, but the crops grown there have not been conclusively identified.

Important Food Plants and Animal Species Domesticated:

Domestication			*Earliest Attested Date of domestication*
Area	*Plants*	*Animals*	
Independent Origin of domestication:			
1. Southwest Asia	wheat, pea, olive	sheep, goat	8,500 B.C.
2. China	rice, millet	pig, silkworm	by 7,500 B.C.
3. Mesoamerica	corn, beans, squash	turkey	by 3,500 B.C.
4. Andes and Amazonia	potato, manioc	llama, guinea pig	by 3,000 B.C.
5. Eastern United States?	sunflower, goosefoot	none	by 2,500 B.C.
6. Sahel	sorghum, African rice	guinea fowl	by 5,000 B.C.

7. Tropical West Africa?	African yams, oil palm	none	by 3,000 B.C.
8. Ethiopia?	coffee, teff	none	by ?
9. New Guinea	sugarcane, banana	none	by 7,000 B.C.
Local Domestication following Arrival of Foundre crops from Elesewhere			
10. Western Europe	poppy, oat	none	by6,000-3,500B.C.
11. Indus Valley	Sesame, eggplant	humped cattle	by 7,000 B.C.
12. Egypt	Sycamore fig, Chufa	donkey, cat,	by 6,000 B.C.
13. Sikkim	Muralimakai,Pangdur, Alainchi,, Ghaiyyadhan, Aduwa, Kankro, Kalobhatmas, Iskus, Silam, buckwheat, Bethu, Sekmuri, Dallekhursani, Marela, Soanp, Dungdugeysag, Lattesag, Rayosag, Suntala.	pig, fowl, dog,	Classic and Post-classic period 300-1500 A.D.

Source: Diamond, J. 1997; Subba, J.R. 2001

13. **Sikkim Himalaya**

Muralimakai, Pangdur, Allainchi, Ghaiyyadhan, Aduwa, Kankro, Kalobhatmas, Iskus, Silam, buckwheat, Bethu, Dallekhursani, Marela, Soanp, Dungdugeysag, Lattesag, Rayosag, Suntala in crops, and pig, fowl, dog, in animals were domesticated latest by the Classic and Postclassic period (c. 300 -1520 A.D.).

The table above summarizes the areas of local domestication of some of the best-known crops and animals and the earliest known dates. Among the nine candidate areas for the independent evolution of food production, Southwest Asia has the earliest established dates for both plant domestication (around 8,500 B.C.) and animal domestication (around 8,000 B.C.); it also has by far the largest number of accurate radiocarbon dates for early food production. Dates for China are nearly as old, while dates for the eastern United States are clearly about 6,000 years later. For the other six candidate areas, none of the earliest well-established dates rival those for Southwest Asia, but too few early sites have been securely dated in these six areas for us to be certain that they really lagged behind Southwest Asia.

The next group of areas consists of ones that did domesticate at least some local plants or animals, but where food production depended mainly on crops and animals that were domesticated elsewhere. The imported domesticates may be taken as "founder" crops and animals because they triggered local food production. The arrival of founder domesticates enabled local people to become sedentary, and thereby increased the likelihood of local crops evolving from wild plants that were gathered, brought home and planted accidentally, and later planted intentionally.

In three or four such areas, the arriving founder package came from Southwest Asia. One of them is western and central Europe, where food production arose with the arrival of Southwest Asian crops and animals between 6,000 and 3,500 B.C., but at least one or two plants were by then domesticated locally. The wild ancestors of most Southwest Asian crops and animals are absent from western Europe. Thus, it seems clear that food production did not evolve independently in western Europe. Instead, it was triggered there by the arrival of Southwest Asian domesticates. The resulting western European farming societies domesticated the poppy, which subsequently spread eastward as a crop.

Another area where local domestication appears to have followed the arrival of Southwest Asian founder crops is the Indus Valley region of the Indian subcontinent. The earliest farming communities there, in the seventh millenium B.C., utilized wheat, barley, and other crops that had been previously domesticated in the Fertile Crescent and that evidently spread to the Indus Valley through Iran. Only later did domesticates derived from indigenous species of the Indian subcontinent, such as the humped cattle and sesame, appear in the Indus Valley farming communities. In Egypt as well, food production began in the sixth millennium B.C. with the arrival of Southwest Asian crops. Egyptians then domesticated the sycamore fig and a local vegetable called chufa.

The same pattern perhaps applies to Ethiopia, where wheat, barley, and other Southwest Asian crops have been cultivated for a long time. Ethiopians also domesticated many locally available wild species, most of which are still confined to Ethiopia. However, it is not yet known whether Ethiopians were cultivating these local plants before or only after the arrival of the Southwest Asian package.

In the Cape of South Africa, the local Khoi hunter-gatherers became herders by acquiring sheep and cows from farther north and ultimately from Southwest Asia. Similarly, native American hunter-gatherers of the U.S. Southwest gradually became farmers by acquiring Mexican crops (Diamond, J. 1997:93-156).

In Sikkim Himalaya, although settled agriculture started only in the last decade of nineteenth century, the inhabiting tribes had domesticated local wild plants such as Kalo bhatmas (*Glycine max*), Pangdur (*Eleusine coracana*), Muralimakai (*Zea mays* var. *everta* Bailey), Kali Makai (*Zea mays* var *indurata*), Ghayya Dhan (*Oryza sativa*), Allainchi (*Amomum subulatum*), Aduwa (*Zingiber officinale*), Kankra (*Cucumis sativus* var. *sikkimensis*), Iskus (*Sechium edule*), Marela (*Memordica balsamina*), Rayosag (*Brasica juncea* var. *folicosa),* Sekmari (*Apium graveolens* var. *dulce*), Dalle Khursani (*Capsicum fruitescens* var. *cerasiforme*), Dungdungey Sag (*Allium porrum*), Methephapar (*Fagopyrum esculentum*), Titeyphapar (*F. tataricum*), Bethu (Chenopodium album), Latte Sag (*Amaranthus caudatus*), Silam (*Perilla frutescens*), Soanp (*Anethum sowa*), and Suntala (*Citrus reticulata*) long before the start of settled agriculture (1890s), probably latest by the Classic and Postclassic Period (c. 300-1520 A.D.).

The primitive mythology of these tribes relate association of many of these local domesticated crops with their own evolution and find a place in their traditions passed down from antiquity even today. Wild plant relatives of these crops are abundant in these areas. The Sikkim Himalaya has been identified as one of the centres of origins of maize (multi-cob bearing popcorn, Primitive maize I & II) by maize scientists. However, it is not yet certain whether the above crops were independently domesticated or, instead, domesticated crops of Chinese origin and Fertile Crescent origin whose arrival triggered the domsetication of the local plants. There is also the possibility that the tribes that inhabited the Sikkim Himalaya migrated from the China region along with the domesticated crops which triggered domestication of local wild plants and animals here.

Thus, we see that only a few areas of the world developed food production independently, and they did so at widely different times. From those nuclear areas, hunter-gathers of some neighbouring areas learned food production, and peoples of other neighbouring areas were replaced by invading food producers from the nuclear areas, again at widely differing times. Also, peoples of some areas ecologically suitable for food production neither evolved nor acquired agriculture in prehistoric times at all. They persisted as hunter-gatherers until the nineteenth century as in the case of the indigenous tribes of Sikkim.

2. What compelled the Hunter-gatherers of the World to adopt Agriculture?

Formerly, all people on earth were hunter-gatherers. Agriculture did not result from a conscious choice made between food production and hunting and gathering. When the first human adopted food production, they could obviously not have been consciously striving towards farming as a goal because they had never seen farming and had no way of knowing what it would be like. Instead, food production evolved as a by-product of decisions made without awareness of the consequences. Many sedentary groups never became food producers while in many areas, mobile groups became food producers. Similarly, in many areas of the world, hunter-gatherers were found the best managers of their land. Food production was developed stepwise. Not all the necessary techniques were developed within a short time and not all the wild plants and animals that were eventually domesticated in a given area were domesticated simultaneously. Even in the cases of the most rapid independent development of food production from a hunting-gathering lifestyle, it took thousands of years to shift from complete dependence on wild foods to a diet with very few domesticated options. In early stages of food production, people simultaneously collected wild foods and raised cultivated ones, and diverse types of collecting activities diminished in importance at different times as reliance on crops increased. The Lepcha and Limboo tribes of Sikkim were at this stage of go-between in the mid-nineteenth century when Dr. J. D. Hooker visited Sikkim in 1849, and described the conditions he found in his book as mentioned in the previous chapter.

The underlying reason for why this transition was piecemeal is that food production systems evolved as a result of accumulation of many separate decisions about allocating time and effort. Foraging humans, like foraging animals, have only finite time and energy which they can allot to different activities. For example, an early farmer waking up and asking: shall I spend today hoeing my garden predictably yielding a lot of vegetables several months from now, or shall I go for fishing predictably yielding a little fish today, or hunting deer yielding possibly a lot of meat today but more likely nothing?

Human and animal foragers are constantly prioritizing and making effort-allocation decisions, even if only unconsciously. These were the questions often asked by an incipient farmer living near the forest, waking up in the morning even before 1890s or even in 2000 A.D. in Sikkim until when the State Government had not notified a total ban on forest and river extraction. They concentrate first on favorite foods, or ones that yield the highest payoff. If these are unavailable, they shift to less and less preferred foods.

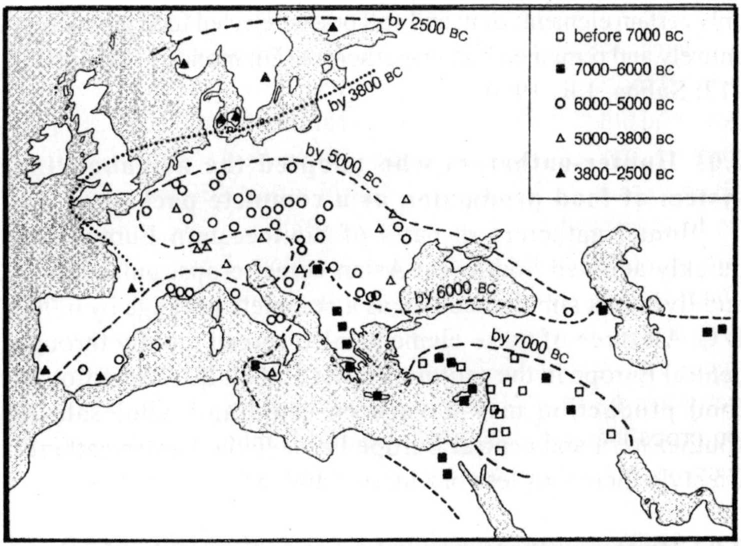

The fertile crescent with early radiocarbon-dated sites

Source: Diamong J. 1997:181

Many considerations enter into these decisions. People in the rural areas seek food in order to satisfy their hunger and fill their bellies. They also crave specific foods, such as protein-rich foods, fat, salt, sweet fruits, and foods that simply taste good. All other things being equal, people seek to maximize their returns of calories, protein, or other specific food categories by foraging in a way that yields the most return with the greatest certainty in the least time for the least effort. Simultaneously, they seek to minimize their risk of starving: moderate but reliable returns are preferable to a fluctuating lifestyle with a high time averaged rate of return but a substantial likelihood of starving to death.

Thus, even though the first farmers in each continent did not choose farming consciously, once food production had arisen in one part of the continent, neighbouring hunter-gatherers could see the results and make conscious decisions. In some cases, the hunter-gatherers adopted the neighbouring system of food production virtually as a complete package; in others, they chose only certain elements of it; and still others rejected food production entirely and remained hunter-gatherers (Diamond, J. 1997:104-112; Subba, J.R. 1984; 2001).

2.01 Hunter-gatherers who adopted the neighbouring system of food production as a complete package:

Hunter-gatherers in parts of Southeastern Europe had quickly adopted Southwest Asian cereal crops, pulse crops, and livestock simultaneously as a complete package by 6,000 B.C. All three of these elements also spread rapidly through central Europe in the centuries before 5,000 B.C. Adoption of food production may have been rapid and wholesale in southeastern and central Europe because the hunter-gatherer lifestyle there was less productive and less competitive.

2.02 Hunter-gathers who adopted only certain elements of Food crops and animals:

In contrast to the above, in Southwestern Europe, namely southern France, Spain, and Italy, food production was adopted piecemeal, with sheep arriving first and cereals later. The adoption of intensive food production from the Asian mainland was also very slow and piecemeal in Japan, probably because the hunter-gather lifestyle based on seafood and local plants was more productive there. Just as a hunting-gathering lifestyle can be traded piecemeal for a food-producing lifestyles, one system of food production can also be traded piecemeal for another. For instance, the natives of the eastern United States were domesticating local plants by about 2,500 B.C. but had trade connections with Mexican Indians who developed a more productive crop system based on the trinity of corn, squash, and beans. Eastern U.S. Indians adopted Mexican crops, and many of them discarded many of their local domesticates piecemeal. Squash was domesticated independently, corn arrived from Mexico around 200 A.D. but remained a minor crop until around 900 A.D., and beans arrived a century or two later.

2.03 Hunter-gatherers who rejected food production entirely:

This type of hunter-gatherers rejected the food production systems in favour of hunting-gathering. For instance, around 3,000 B.C. the hunter-gatherers of southern Sweden adopted farming based on Southwest Asian crops, but abandoned it around 2,700 B.C. and reverted to hunting-gathering for 400 years before resuming farming.

Thus, it is clear that the decision to adopt farming was not made in a vacuum, as if the people previously had no means to feed themselves. Instead, we must consider food production and hunting-gathering as alternative strategies competing with each other. Mixed farming that added certain crops or livestock to hunting-gathering also competed against both types of "pure" farming, and against mixed farming with higher or lower proportions of food production. For instance, in the nineteenth century A.D., the hunter-gathers of Sikkim were at a stage of finding food production and hunting-gathering alternatives; while in the twentieth century they were in search of mixed farming with higher or lower proportions of food production. However, over the last 10,000 years, the predominant result has been a shift from hunting-gathering to food production (Diamond, J. 1997:104-112; Subba, J.R. 1984; 2001).

3.00 Factors for adaptation of food production:

Diamond J. (1997) has pointed out five important factors that compelled the hunter-gatherers for adaptation of food production. They are:

3.01 Decline in the availability of wild foods:

The lifestyle of hunter-gatherers has become increasingly less rewarding over the past 13,000 years as resources on which they depended, especially animal resources, became less abundant and in some cases even disappeared. Most of the large mammal species became extinct in North and South America at the end of Pleistocene, and some went extinct in Eurasia and Africa, either because of climate change or because of the rise in skill and numbers of human hunters. Similarly, the numbers of wild gazelles that had previously been a major source of meat for hunter-gatherers of the Fertile Crescent had declined, contributing one of the factors for animal domestication in that area.

3.02 Availability of domesticable wild plants:

Just as the depletion of wild game tended to make hunting-gathering less rewarding, an increased availability of domesticable wild plants made steps leading to plant domestication more rewarding. For instance, climate change at the end of the Pleistocene in the Fertile Crescent greatly expanded the habitat for wild cereals, of which huge crops could be harvested in a short time. These wild cereal wheat and barley harvests were precursors to the domestication of the earliest crops in the Fertile Crescent.

3.03 Cumulative Development of Technologies of Food Production:

Still another factor tipping the balance away from hunting-gathering was the cumulative development of technologies on which food production would eventually depend, technologies for collecting, processing, and storing wild foods. The necessary methods, implements, and facilities for wheat and barley harvesting, processing and storing appeared rapidly in the Fertile Crescent after 11,000 B.C., invented for dealing with the newly available abundance of wild cereals. All these techniques, though developed for the exploitation of wild cereals, were prerequisites to the planting of cereals as crops. These cumulative developments of sickles of flint blades cemented into wooden or bone handles for harvesting wild grains; baskets for collection and carriage from the hillsides where they grew; mortars and pestles, or grinding slabs to remove the husks; the technique of roasting grains so that they could be stored without sprouting; and underground storage pits, some plastered to make them waterproof etc. constituted the unconscious first steps of plant domestication.

3.04 Two-way link between the rise in human population density and the rise in food production:

In all parts of the world where adequate evidence is available, archaeologists find evidence of rising densities associated with the appearance of food production. This is a long-debated chicken-or-egg enigma: did a rise in human population density force people to turn to food production, or did food production permit a rise in population density?

In principle, one expects the chain of causation to operate in both directions. Food production tends to lead to increased population densities because it yields more edible calories per acre than hunting-gathering. On the other hand, human population densities were gradually rising throughout the late Pleistocene anyway thanks to improvements in human technology for collecting and processing wild foods. As population densities rose, food production became increasingly favoured because it provided the increased food outputs required to feed all those people.

3.05 The Final Decisive Factor:

A final factor became decisive in the establishing of geographical boundaries between hunter-gatherers and food producers. The much denser populations of food producers enabled them to displace or kill hunter-gatherers with their sheer numbers, not to mention the other advantages associated with food production. In areas where there were only hunter-gatherers to begin with, those groups of hunter-gatherers who adopted food production out bred those who didn't.

As a result, in most areas of the globe suitable for food production, hunter-gatherers met one of two fates: either they were displaced by neighbouring food producers, or they survived only by adopting food production themselves. However, in many places, food producers replaced the hunter-gatherers in the prehistoric era. Those few peoples who remained hunter-gatherers into the 20th century escaped replacement by food producers because they were confined to areas not fit for food production (Ibid:104-112).

4.00 Wild Plants domestication for Food production:

The earliest wild plants such as the Wheat, Barley and Peas which were domesticated around 10,000 years ago in the Fertile Crescent arose from wild ancestors offering many advantages. They were already edible and gave high yields in the wild. They could be easily grown, merely by being sown or planted. They grew quickly and could be harvested within a few months of sowing, a big advantage for incipient farmers still on the borderline between being nomadic hunters to becoming settled villagers. They could be readily stored, unlike many later crops. They were mostly self-pollinating and finally, their wild ancestors required very little genetic change to be converted into crops, for instance, in wheat, just the mutations for non-shattering stalks and uniform quick germination.

The next stage of crop development included the first fruit and nut trees domesticated around 4,000 B.C. These comprised of olives (Mediterranean region), fig, dates, pomegranates, and grapes (Eurasia). Compared with cereals and legumes, they had the drawback of not starting to yield food until at least three years after planting, and not reaching full production until as much as a decade later. Thus, growing these crops was possible only for people already fully committed to settled village life. However, these early fruit and nut trees were still the easiest such crops to cultivate. Unlike later tree domesticates; they could be grown directly by being planted as cuttings or even seeds.

The third stage involved fruit trees that proved much harder to cultivate, including apples (Eurasia), pears, plums, and cherries. These trees cannot be grown from cuttings. It's also a waste of effort to grow them from seeds since the offspring even of an outstanding individual tree of there species are highly variable and mostly yield worthless fruit. Instead, these trees must be grown through the difficult technique of grafting, developed in China long after the beginning of agriculture. Many of these late-stage fruit trees posed a further problem in that their wild progenitors were the opposite of self-pollinating. They had to be cross-pollinated by another plant belonging to a genetically different variety of their species. Hence, early farmers either had to find mutant trees not requiring cross-pollination or had to consciously plant genetically different varieties or else male and female individuals nearby in the same orchard. All these problems delayed the domestication of apples, pears, plums, and cherries until around the classical times. At about that same time, crops starting out as weeds included rye and oats, turnips and radish, beets and leeks, and lettuce.

Cereal crops have the virtue of being fast growing, high in carbohydrates and yielding up to a tonne of edible food per hectare. As a result, cereals today account for over half of all calories consumed by humans and include five of the modern world's 12 leading crops (Wheat, corn, rice, barley, and sorghum). Many cereal crops are low in protein, but pulses, which are often 25 percent protein, make up that deficit. Cereals and pulses together thus provide many of the ingredients of a balanced diet (Ibid:104-112).

Early Major Crops Types domesticated by the Farmers around the Ancient World:

Area	*Cereals other grasses*	*Pulses*	*Fiber*	*Roots & Tubers, melons*
Fertile Crescent	emmer wheat, einkorn wheat,	pea, lentil, chickpes barley.	flax	muskmelon
China	foxtail millet,	soybean, broomcorn millet, rice	hemp	muskmelon adzuki bean, mung bean
Mesoamerica	corn	common bean,	cotton	jicama,
		tepary bean, scarlet runner bean,	(*hirsutum*), yucca, agave	squash (*C. pepo*)
Andes,	quinoa,	lima bean,	cotton	manioc,
Amazonia	(corn)	common bean, peanut	(*barba-dense*)	sweet potato, squash (*C. maxima*) potato, oca.
West Africa and Sahel	sorghum, pearl millet, African rice	cowpea, groundnut.	cotton (*herbaceum*)	African yams, watermelon, bottle gourd.
India	(wheat, barley, rice, sorghum, millet)	hyacinth bean, black gram, green gram	cotton (*arboreum*), flax	cucumber
Ethiopia	teff, fingermillet, (wheat, barley)	(pea, lentil)	(flax)	
Eastern United States	maygrass, little barley, knotweed, goosefoot			Jerusalem artichoke squash (*C. pepo*)
New Guinea	sugarcane			yam, taro

Brackets crops first domesticated elsewhere.

Source: Diamond J. 1997: 126-7.

The domestication of local cereal-pulse combination launched food production in many areas. The most familiar examples are the combination of wheat and barley with peas and lentils in the Fertile Crescent, corn with several bean species in Mesoamerica, and the combination of rice and millet with soybeans and other beans in China. Less well known are Africa's combination of sorghum, African rice, and pearl millet with cowpeas and groundnuts, and the Andes' combination of the non-cereal grain quinoa with several bean species. The Fertile Crescent's early domestication of flax for fiber was paralleled elsewhere. Hemp, four cotton species, yucca, and agave variously furnished fiber for rope and woven clothing in China, Mesoamerica, India, Ethiopia, sub-Saharan Africa, and South America, supplemented in several of those areas by wool from domestic animals. Of the centres of early food production, only the eastern United States and New Guinea remained without a fiber crop.

Although these parallels existed, there were also some major differences in food production systems around the world. One is that agriculture in much of the Old World came to involve broadcast seeding and monoculture fields, and eventually ploughing. That is, seeds were sown thrown in handfuls resulting in a whole field devoted to a single crop. Once cows, horses, and other large mammals were domesticated, they were hitched to ploughs and fields were tilled by animal power. In the New World, however, no animal was ever domesticated that could be hitched to a plow. Instead, hand-held sticks or hoes tilled fields and seeds were planted individually by hand and not scattered as whole handfuls. Most New World fields thus came to be mixed gardens of many crops planted together, rather than monoculture.

Another major difference among agricultural systems involved the main sources of calories and carbohydrates. Cereals were important sources of calories and carbohydrates in the Fertile Crescent and China, cassava and sweet potato were staples in Tropical South America, potato and oca in the Andes, African yams in Africa, and Indo-Pacific yams and taro in Southeast Asia and New Guinea. Tree crops, notably bananas and breadfruit, also furnished carbohydrate-rich staples in Southeast Asia and New Guinea (Diamond, J. 1997:114-156; Subba, J.R. 1984; 1995; 2001).

5. The Importance of the Modern World's Crops Today:

Of the 200,000 or more wild plant species, only a few thousand are eaten by humans, and just a few hundred of these have been more or less domesticated. Even of these several hundred crops, most provide minor supplements to our diet and would not by themselves have sufficed to support the rise of civilizations. A mere dozen species account for over 80 percent of the modern world's annual tonnage of crops. Those dozen blockbusters are the cereals wheat, corn, rice, barley, and sorghum; the pulse soybean; the root or tubers potato, cassava, and sweet potato; the sugar sources sugarcane and sugar beet; and the fruit banana. Cereal crops alone now account for more than half of the calories consumed by the world's human populations. With such few major crops in the world, all domesticated thousands of years ago, and hardly any wild native plants of outstanding potential left, our failure to domesticate even a single major new food plant in modern times suggests that ancient peoples must have explored virtually all useful wild plants and domesticated all the ones worth domesticating.

Domestication of wild plants and animal species depends on two factors. The first is the availability of suitable wild plants or animals; and the second would lie in cultural characteristics of the people. At least some humans must have been receptive to the experimentation that led to domestication of wild plants and animals.

One of the central facts of human history is the early importance of the part of Southwest Asia known as the Fertile Crescent (because of the crescent-like shape of it uplands on a map). This area appears to have been the earliest site for a whole string of developments, including cities, writing, empires, and what we term civilizations. All these developments sprang, in turn, from the dense human populations, stored food surpluses, and feeding of non-farming specialists made possible by the rise of food production in the form of crop cultivation and animal husbandry. Food production was the first of these major innovations to appear in the Fertile Crescent. Hence, any attempt to understand the origins of the modern world must come to grips with the question of why the Fertile Crescent's domesticated plants and animals gave it such a potent head start.

One advantage of the Fertile Crescent is that it lies within a zone of so-called Mediterranean climate, a climate characterized by mild, wet winters and long, hot, dry summers. That climate selects for plant species able to survive the long dry season and to resume growth rapidly upon the return of the rains. Many Fertile Crescent plants, especially the cereals and pulses, have adopted in a way that renders them useful to humans; they are annuals, meaning that the plant itself dries up and dies in the dry season. Within their mere one year lifespan, annual plants inevitably remain small herbs. Many of them put much of their energy into producing big seeds, which remain dormant during the dry season and are then ready to sprout when the rains come. Annual plants therefore waste little energy on making inedible wood or fibrous stems, like the body of trees and bushes. But many of the big seeds, notably those of the annual cereals, and pulses are edible. They constitute six of the modern world's 12 major crops.

The second advantage of the Fertile Crescent flora is that the wild ancestors of many Fertile Crescent crops were already abundant and highly productive, occurring in large strands whose value must have been obvious to hunter-gatherers of that area around 10,000 years ago. By collecting huge quantities of wild cereals and pulses (wheat, barlet, peas) in a short time when the seeds were ripe, and storing them for use as food through the rest of the year, some hunting-gathering peoples of that area had already settled down in permanent villages even before they began to cultivate plants.

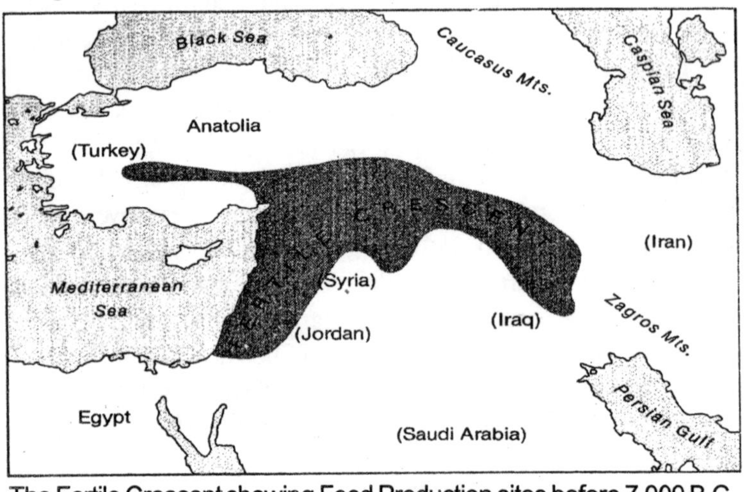

The Fertile Crescent showing Food Production sites before 7,000 B.C.

Source: Diamond J. 1997: 135

A third advantage of the Fertile Crescent flora is that it includes a high percentage of hermaphrodittic "selfers", that is, plants that usually pollinate themselves but that are occasionally cross-pollinated. Such crops were also convenient for early farmers in that they occasionally did become cross-pollinated, thereby generating new varieties to select from.

Thus, agriculture was launched in the Fertile Crescent with the domestication of eight crops, termed "founder crops". These eight founder crops were the cereals emmer wheat, einkorn wheat, and barley; pulses lentil, pea, chickpea, and bitter vetch; and the fiber crop flax. Of the eight, only two, flax and barley, range in the wild outside the Fertile Crescent and Anatolia. Two of the founder crops had very small ranges in the wild, chickpea being confined to southeastern Turkey and emmer wheat to the Fertile Crescent itself. Thus, agriculture could arise in the Fertile Crescent from domestication of locally available wild plants, without having to wait for the arrival of crops derived from wild plants domesticated elsewhere. Conversely, two of the eight founder crops could not have been domesticated anywhere in the world except in the Fertile Crescent, since they did not occur in the wild anywhere else.

The hunter-gatherers of the Fertile Crescent could thus quickly assemble a potent and balanced biological package for intensive food production. This package comprised of three cereals (emmer wheat, einkorn wheat, barley), as the main carbohydrate sources; four pulses (pea, lentil, chickpea, bitter vetch), with 20-25 percent protein, and four domestic animals (sheep, goat, pig, cow), as the main protein sources, supplemented by generous protein content of wheat; and flax as a source of fiber and oil (termed linseed oil: flax seeds are about 40 percent oil). Eventually, thousands of years after the beginning of animal domestication and food production, the animals were also used for milk, wool, plowing, and transport. Thus, the crops and animals of the Fertile Crescent's first farmers came to meet humanity's basic economic needs - carbohydrate, protein, fat, clothing, traction, and transport. The food production package of the Fertile Crescent must have faced hardly any competition from the hunter-gatherer lifestyles because of reduced availability of meat from gazelle, and the food package quickly became superior to the hunter-gatherer package. By 6,000 B.C. some societies there were almost completely dependent on crops and domestic animals (Ibid:114-156; Subba, J.R. 1984; 1995; 2001).

6. Domestication of Wild Animals:

The big domesticated mammals were crucial to human societies possessing them. They provided meat, milk products, manure, transport, leather, military assault vehicles, plow traction, and wool, as well as germs that killed previously unexposed peoples. In addition, of course, small domestic animals and domestic birds and insects have also been useful to humans. Many birds were domesticated for meat, eggs, and feathers: the chicken in China and the Himalayan region of Nepal and India, various duck and goose species in parts of Eurasia, turkeys in Mesoamerica, guinea fowl in Africa, and the Muscovy duck in South America. Wolves were domesticated in Eurasia and North America to become our dogs used as hunting companions, sentinels, pets, and, in some societies, food. Rodents and other small mammals domesticated for food included the rabbit in Europe, the guinea pig in the Andes, giant rat in West Africa, and possibly a rodent called the hutia in the Caribbean islands. Ferrets were domesticated in Europe to hunt rabbits, and cats were domesticated in North Africa and Southwest Asia to hunt rodent pests. Even some insects have been domesticated, notably Eurasia's honeybee and China's silkworm moth, kept for honey and silk respectively. Only terrestrial mammals have been domesticated, for the obvious reason that aquatic mammals were difficult to maintain and breed until the development of modern Sea World facilities.

If one defines "big" as weighting over 100 lbs., then only 14 such species were domesticated before the twentieth century. Of these Ancient Fourteen, nine became important livestock for people in only limited areas of the globe. These are the Arabian camel, Bactrian camel, llama/ alpaca, donkey, reindeer, water buffalo, yak, banteng, and gaur. Only five species became widespread and important around the world. The Major Five of mammal domestication are the cow, sheep, goat, pig, and horse (Diamond, J. 1997:157-175).

6.1 The Ancient Fourteen Species of Big Herbivorous Domestic Mammals:

The Major Five:

1. Sheep: domesticated around 8,000 B.C. in the Southwest Asia. Wild ancestor: the Asiatic mouflon sheep of west and central Asia. Now worldwide.
2. Goat: domesticated around 8,000 B.C. in the Southwest Asia. Wild ancestor: the bezoar goat of west Asia. Now worldwide.
3. Cow, alias ox or cattle: domesticated around 6,000 B.C. in the Southwest Asia, India, (?) North Africa. Wild ancestor: the extinct aurochs, formerly distributed over Eurasia and North Africa. Now worldwide.
4. Pig: Wild ancestor: the wild boar, distributed over Eurasia and North Africa. Now worldwide. Actually an omnivore, whereas the other 13 of the Ancient Fourteen are more strictly herbivores.
5. Horse: domesticated around 4,000 B.C. in Ukraine. Wild ancestor: now extinct wild horses of southern Russia; a different subspecies of the same species survived in the wild upto modern times as Przewalski's horse of Mongolia. Now worldwide.

The Minor Nine:

6. Arabian (one-humped) camel: domesticated around 2,500 B.C. in Arabia. Wild ancestor: now extinct, formerly lived in Arabia and adjacent areas. Still largely restricted to Arabia and northern Africa, though feral in Australia.
7. Bactrian (two-humped) camel: domesticated around 2,500 B.C. in Central Asia. Wild ancestor: now extinct, lived in Central Asia. Still largely confined to Central Asia.
8. Llama and alpaca: domesticated around 3,500 B.C. in Andes. These appear to be well-differentiated breeds of the same species, rather than different species. Wild ancestor: the guanaco

of the Andes. Still largely confined to the Andes, although some are bred as pack animals in North America.

9. Donkey: domesticated around 4,000 B.C. in Egypt. Wild ancestor: the African wild ass of North Africa, and Sikkim Himalaya and formerly perhaps the adjacent area of Southwest Asia. Originally confined as a domestic animal to North Africa and western Eurasia, more recently also used elsewhere.
10. Reindeer: Wild ancestor: the reindeer of northern Eurasia. Still largely confined as a domestic animal to that area, though now some are also used in Alaska.
11. Water buffalo: Wild ancestor lives in Southeast Asia. Still used as a domestic animal mainly in that area, though many are also used in Brazil and other have escaped to the wild in Australia and other places.
12. Yak: Wild ancestor: the wild yak of the Himalayas and Tibetan plateau. Still confined as a domestic animal to that area.
13. Bali cattle: Wild ancestor: the banteng (a relative of the aurochs) of Southeast Asia. Still confined as a domestic animal of that area.
14. Mithan: Wild ancestor: the gaur (another relative of the aurochs) of Indian and Burma. Still confined as a domestic animal to that area.

The wild ancestors of the Ancient Fourteen were spread unevenly across the globe. South America had only one such ancestor, which gave rise the llama and alpaca. North America, Australia, and sub-Saharan Africa had none at all. The lack of domestic mammals indigenous to sub-Saharan Africa is specially astonishing, since a main reason why tourists visit Africa today is to see its abundance and diverse wild mammals. In contrast, the wild ancestors of 13 of the Ancient Fourteen (including the Major Five) were confined to Eurasia. Of course, not all 13 of these wild ancestal species occurred throughout Eurasia. No area had all 13 and some of the wild ancestors were quite local, such as the yak, confined in the wild to Tibet and adjacent highland areas. However, many parts of Eurasia did have quite a few of these 13 species living in the same area: for example, seven of the wild ancestors occurred in Southwest Asia.

Mammal Candidates for Domestication:

	Continents			
	Eurasia	*Sub-Saharan Africa*	*The America*	*Australia*
Candidates	72	51	24	1
Domesticated species	13	0	1	0
Percentage domesticated	18%	0%	4%	0%

Source: Diamond, J. 1997:114-156

Eurasia becoming the main site of big mammal domestication stems from its advantage of being the continent with the most candidate species of wild mammals to start out with. It also lost the fewest candidates to extinction in the last 40,000 years. It is also because of the other five factors such as: rapid acceptance of Eurasian domesticates by non-Eurasian peoples, the universal human penchant for keeping pets, the rapid domestication of the Ancient Fourteen, the repeated independent domestications of some of them, and the limited success of modern efforts at further domestications.

All species for whom dates of domestication have archaeological evidence were domesticated between about 8,000 and 2,000 B.C., that is, within the first few thousand years of the sedentary farming-herding societies that arose with the end of the last Ice Age. The era of big mammal domestication began with the sheep, goat, and pig and ended with camels. Since 2,500 B.C., there have been no significant additions. However, some small mammals were domesticated long after 2,500 B.C.

7. Factors of Domestication:

In all, of the world's 148 big wild terrestrial herbivorous mammals, only 14 species passed the test of domestication. 134 species failed for domestication because of the following factors:

7.1 Diet:

The domesticated animal species are mostly herbivores due to their conversion of food biomass into the consumer's biomass efficiency, which is typically around 10 percent. As a result of this fundamental inefficiency of herbivores, no mammalian carnivore has ever been domesticated for food.

7.2 Growth Rate:

To be worth keeping, domesticates must also grow quickly.

7.3 Problems of Captive Breeding:

Some potentially valuable animal species don't like to have sex under the watchful eyes of others, for example, cheetahs.

7.4 Nasty Disposition:

Naturally, almost any mammal species that is sufficiently large is capable of killing a human. Some large animals have much nastier dispositions and are more incurably dangerous than are others. Tendencies to kill humans have disqualified many otherwise seemingly ideal candidates for domestication.

7.5 Tendency to Panic:

Big mammalian herbivore species react to danger from predators or humans in different ways. The nervous species are difficult to keep in captivity. If put into an enclosure, they are likely to panic, and either die of shock or batter themselves to death against the fence in their attempts to escape.

7.6 Social Structure:

Social structure is ideal for domestication, because humans in effect take over the dominant hierarchy. Social animals lend themselves to herding. In contrast, members of most solitary territorial animal species cannot be herded and thus cannot be domesticated (Ibid:114-156).

8. Spread of Food Production/ Agriculture:

The basic feature of geography, that is axis orientations

affected the rate of spread of crops and livestock in the last 500 years. There were no more than nine areas of the globe, perhaps even as few as five, where food production developed independently. Yet, already in prehistoric times, food production became established in many other regions besides those few areas of origins.

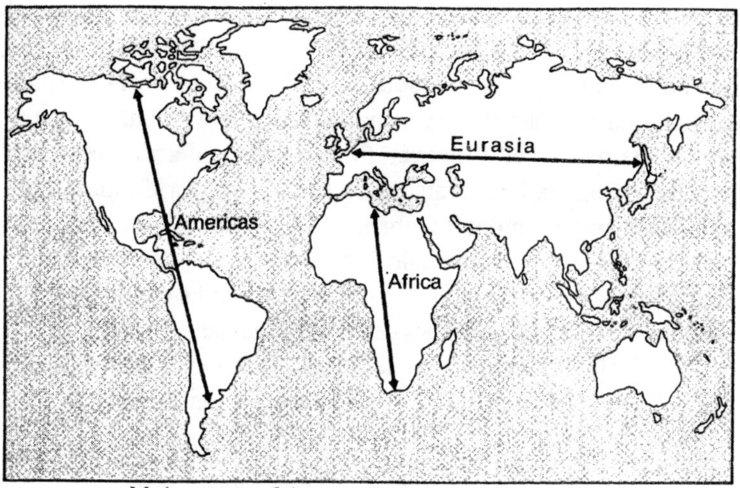

Major axes of the continents (Source:Ibid)

All those other areas became food producing as a result of the spread of crops, livestock, and knowledge of how to grow them and, in some cases, as a result of migrations of farmers and herders themselves. The main such spreads of food production were from Southwest Asia to Europe, Egypt and North Africa to East and South Africa; from China to tropical Southeast Asia, the Philippines, Indonesia, Korea, and Japan; and from Mesoamerica to North America. Moreover, food production even in the areas of origin became enriched with the addition of crops, livestock, and techniques from other areas of origin.

Many of the Fertile Crescent's founder crops don't even occur in the wild outside Southwest Asia. For instance, none of the eight main founder crops except barley grows wild in Egypt. Egypt's Nile Valley provides an environment similar to the Fertile Crescent's Tigris and Euphrates Valleys. Hence the package that worked well in the latter valleys also worked well enough in the Nile Valley to trigger the spectacular rise of the Egyptian civilization. But the foods to fuel that spectacular rise were originally absent in Egypt. The sphinx and pyramids were built by people fed on crops originally native to the Fertile Crescent, not to Egypt.

Even for those crops whose wild ancestors occur outside of Southwest Asia, we can be confident that the crops of Europe and India were mostly obtained from Southwest Asia and were not local domesticates. For example, wild flax occurs west to Britain and Algeria and east to the Caspian Sea, while wild barley occurs east even up to Tibet. However, for most of the Fertile Crescent's founding crops, all cultivated varieties in the world today share only one arrangement of chromosomes out of the multiple arrangements found in the wild ancestor; or else they share only a single mutation by which the cultivated varieties differ from the wild ancestor in characteristics desirable to humans. Evidently, most of the Fertile Crescent's founder crops were never domesticated again elsewhere after their initial domestication there (Ibid:114-156).

9. Food Production in mountainous Sikkim

Agriculturally, food production in mountainous Sikkim can be divided into five periods as follows:

9.1 Period of Shifting cultivation (Antiquity to 1890 A.D.)

This period marks the beginning of food production with the founder crops domesticated elsewhere in the mountainous region of China, India and the Fertile Cresant such as finger millet, barley, dryland paddy, primitive maize, soybean, mungbean, ricebean etc. under slash and burn condition or shifting cultivation. The farmers also domesticated the local wild plants and animals. The local domesticates were: *Murolimakai, Pangdur, Allainchi, Ghaiyyadhan, Aduwa, Kankro, Kalobhatmas, Iskus, Silam,* *buckwheat, Bethu, Dallekhursani, Marela, Soanp, Dungdugeysag, Lattesag, Rayosag, Suntala* in crops and pig, fowl, dog, in animals latest by the Classic and Postclassic period

(c. 300 -1520 A.D.). Due to low density of population and the area being rich in biodiversity of plants and animals, hunting gathering was more paying than food production for the people in the initial period.

9.2 Period of Settled Agriculture (1890-1953 A.D.)

Settled agriculture with bench terracing of sloppy lands of mountainous Sikkim debuted in the 1890s with the British policy of promoting Nepalese settlements in Sikkim; this, initially to raise State funds needed for development and solve the labour requirement for trade. Settled agriculture food production accelerated with the introduction of irrigated paddy cultivation, fingermillet transplanting system etc. A large number of crops and crop-varieties such as maize, paddy, other millets, wheat, rape and mustard, and livestock such as milch cattle, buffalo, goat, sheep, pig, poultry birds etc. were introduced during this period.

9.3 Period of Planning and Development (under Chiefdomship 1954-1975 A.D.)

With the initiation of the Five Year Plans in 1954, economic development started on the lines of India with the assistance of Government of India during this period in Chiefdom. Guava Seed Production Farm, Hilley Potato Farm and Tadong Veternary Farm were established for seed selection and multiplication. A large number of improved crop varieties and improved breeds of livestock were introduced, conducted adaptive trials, multiplied the better onces and distributed to the farmers for food production.

9.4 Period of Intensive Agriculture (Under Statehood 1976-2002 A.D.)

Sikkim was integrated as the 22nd State of India in 1975. The State adopted the regional concept of agricultural development and divided the State into 9 regions and 7 sub-regions each having seed multiplication farms for seed multiplication and distribution to the farmers. A large number of improved and hybrid seeds were introduced for cultivation. Use of fertilazer and pesticides was at the maximum during this period. A number of improved and hybrid livestock were also introduced leading to intensive agriculture with mixed farming. As a result, the sloppy lands of mountainous Sikkim were eroded, natural resource-base depleted, and productivity declined.

9.5 Period of Organic Agriculture (2003 A.D...)

The State Government realized that Sikkim being a mountainous region has no scope for intensive agriculture. Hence, the policy of organic agriculture was adopted. This facilitates low/ slow use of natural resource-base and also provides ample scope for conservation and regeneration of natural resources. Thus, the State has adopted stall-fed livestock and precision farming with green house cultivation, drip irrigation, organic composting for growing organic high-value horticultural crops based on regional comparative advantages.

The area, production and productivity of the crops and livestock are as follows:

Crops	*Particulars*	*1975-76*	*1980-81*	*1990-91*	*2000-01*	*2004-05*
Rice	A	11.40	14.80	16.05	15.21	14.74
	P	10.00	10.60	16.05	21.35	21.61
	Pr	877	718	1373	1403	1466
Wheat	A	0.15	8.85	7.82	7.21	5.74
	P	0.15	13.21	13.08	10.10	8.25
	Pr	1000	1493	1673	1400	1437
Maize	A	28.50	30.20	39.90	39.90	36.70
	P	16.5	28.93	57.60	59.61	58.19
	Pr	579	959	1444	1494	1585
Barley	A	0.90	0.58	0.90		
	P	0.50	0.46	1.18		
	Pr	556	793	1311		
Buckwheat	A	1.50	2.76	1.72		
	P	0.80	1.38	1.42		
	Pr	533	500	825		
Fingermillet	A	4.80	5.00	4.90		

	P	3.20	3.84	4.62		
	Pr	667	768	943		
Other cereals	A				7.69	7.39
	P				6.97	6.68
	Pr				906	904
Total cereals	A	47.25	62.19	71.29	70.01	71.96
	P	31.15	54.46	99.94	110.57	108.73
	Pr	659	940	1402	1400	1316
Pulses	A	1.70	4.40	6.13	6.03	6.71
(urd & others)	P	0.70	3.32	5.43	5.16	6.44
	Pr	412	755	88	857	950
Total food	A	48.95	66.59	77.42	86.03	88.62
	P	31.85	61.77	105.37	110.57	108.73
	Pr	651	928	1361	1285	1227

A, P and Pr = Area ('000 ha), Production ('000 tonnes) and Productivity (kg/ha).

Source: Subba, J.R. 2001; 2006

The major livestock products in 2001 were milk 37,000 million tonnes, meat 3,500 million tonnes of which poultry meat constituted 500 million tonnes; eggs 10.03 million, contributing 8.16 per cent of GSDP of the State.

The State is not self-sufficient in food and sources about 46,000 tonnes of rice and wheat alone and about 800 tonnes of meat from other states annually as on 2004.

The major crops grown are maize, paddy, wheat, barley, fingermillet, buckwheat in cereals; blackgram, horsegram, ricebean, fieldpeas and fieldbeans in pulses; soybean, rape and mustard in oilseeds; potato, sweetpotato, cassava, colocasia, greater yams in root and tubers; large cardamom, ginger, turmeric in spices; orange, apple, banana, guava, avocado, papaya, peach, plum, pear in fruits; radish, pumpkin, chayote, tree tomato, cauliflower, cabbage, tomato, chilly, peas, beans, cowpea, turnip, carrot, bottlegourd, spongegourd, snakegourd, bittergourd, cucumber, balsum apple, palak, amaranthus, leafy mustard, leek, garlick, fenugreek, etc. in vegetables. The major livestock are miltch cattle, buffalo, sheep, goat, pig and poultry (Subba, J.R. 1984; 1995; 2001; 2002; 2006).

3
Writing System

On July 3rd 2007, I had the opportunity to visit the "Metropolitan Museum of Art" at New York. True to its status as the largest museum in the world, the "Met" collection, spanning the entire history of artistic expression, is the centerpiece of "Museum Mile", an astounding repository of world-class galleries extending along the eastern side of Central Park and South along 5th Avenue. The museum is an enormous public artistic heritage accumulation. In this museum, I had the opportunity to see closely the famous Babylonian cuneiform writing specimen on round can-like Terracotta derived from Sumerian cuneiform.

The history of progression of human beings from hunting-gathering (savagery) to civilization includes the development of agriculture, metallurgy, complex technology, centralized government, and writing. Of these, writing was traditionally the most restricted geographically until the expansions of Islam and of colonial Europeans. It was absent from Australia, Pacific islands, subequatorial Africa, and the whole New World except for a small part of Mesoamerica. As a result of this confined circulation, people who prides themselves as being civilized have always viewed writing as the sharpest distinction raising them above "barbarians" or "savages".

Knowledge brings power; and writing brings power to modern societies, by making it possible to transmit knowledge with far greater accuracy and in far greater quantity and detail, from more distant lands and more remote times. Writing marched together with weapons, microbes, and centralized political organization as a modern agent of conquest (Diamond, J. 1997:215-264; Sacks, David 2003).

1. The basic strategies of writing systems:

The three basic strategies underlying writing systems differ in the size of the speech unit denoted by one written sign, such as a single basic sound, a whole syllable, or a whole word. Of these, the one employed nowadays by most people is the alphabet, which ideally would provide a unique sign (termed a letter) for each basic sound of the language (a phoneme) (e. g. the English alphabet). The second strategy uses so-called logograms, meaning that one written sign stands for a whole word (e. g. Chinese writing and Japanese/ kanji writing system). Before the spread of alphabetic writing, systems making much use of logograms were more common and included Egyptian hieroglyphs (as also Hiratic and Debhotic), Maya glyphs, Indus Valley Picto-phonographic and Sumerian cuneiform. The third strategy, uses a sign for each syllable. In practice, most such writing systems (termed syllabaries) provide distinct signs just for syllables of one consonant followed by one vowel (like the syllables of the word "family"), and resort to various tricks in order to write other types of syllables by means of those signs. Syllabaries were common in ancient times, as exemplified by the Linear B writing of Mycenaean Greece. Some syllabaries still persist , the most important being the kana syllabaries that the Japanese use for telegrams, bank statements, and texts for blind readers. In practice, no actual writing system employs one strategy exclusively. Chinese writing is not purely logographic, nor is English writing purely alphabetic. Like all alphabetic writing systems, English uses many logograms, such as numerical, $, %, and +: that is arbitrary signs, not made up of phonetic elements, representing whole words. "Syllabic" Linear B had many logograms, and "logographic" Egyptian hieroglyphs included many syllabic signs as well as a virtual alphabet of individual letters for each consonant (Diamond, J. 1997:215-264; Sacks, David 2003).

2. Inventing a writing system:

Inventing a writing system from the scratch must have been incomparably more difficult than borrowing and adapting one. The first scribes had to settle on basic principles that we now take for granted. For example, they had to figure out how to decompose a continuous utterance into speech units, regardless of whether those units were taken as words, syllables, or phonemes. They had to learn to recognize the same sound or speech unit through all our normal variations in speech volume, pitch, speed, emphasis, phrase grouping, and individual idiosyncrasies of pronunciation. They had to decide that a writing system should ignore all of that variation. They than had to devise ways to represent sounds by symbols.

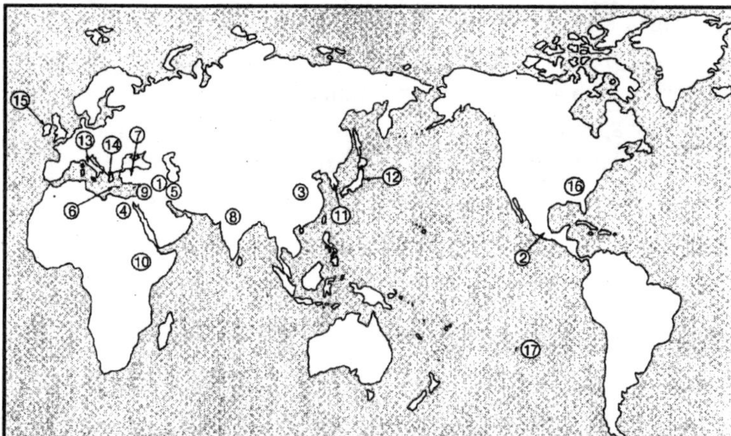

a) Independent or possibly independent origins: 1. Sumer, 2. Mesoamerica, ?3. China, ??4.Egypt; b) Other: 5. Proto-Elamite, 7. Hittite, 8. Indus Valley, 17. Easter Island; c) Syllabaries: 6. Crete (Linear A and B), 12. Japan (kana), 16. Cherokee; d) Alphabets: 9. West Semitic, Phoenician, 10. Ethiopian, 11. Korea (han'gol), 13. Italy (Roman, Etruscan), 14. Greece, 15. Ireland (ogham).

Source: Diamond, J. 1997:219.

Somehow, the first scribes solved all these problems, without having recourse to any examples of the final result to guide their efforts. That task was evidently so difficult that there have been only a few occasions in history when people invented writing systems entirely on their own. The few indisputably independently inventions of writing were achieved by the Sumerians of Mesopotamia sometime before 3,000 B.C., Egyptian of 3,200 B.C., Chinese of

2,800 B.C. Indus Valley Picto-Phonographic script of 2,600 B.C. and by Mexican Indians before 600 B.C. Probably all other peoples who have developed writing since than have borrowed, adapted, or at least been inspired by existing systems.

The independent invention that we can trace in greatest detail is history's oldest writing system, Ancient Sumerian cuneiform. The earliest Sumerian writings consisted of non-phonetic logogram. That is to say, it was not based on the specific sounds of the Sumerian languages, and it could have been pronounced with entirely different sounds to yield the same meaning in any other language, just as the numerical sign 4 is variously pronounced four, *chetwire, nelja*, and *empat* by speakers of English, Russian, Finnish, and Indonesian, respectively, but means the same number in all these tongues. Perhaps the most important single step in the whole history of writing was the Sumerians' introduction of phonetic representation, initially by writing an abstract noun by means of the sign for a depictable noun that had the same phonetic pronunciation. For instance, it's easy to draw a recognizable picture of *arrow*; hard to draw a recognizable picture of *life*, but both are pronounced *ti* in Sumerian, so a picture of an arrow came to mean either *arrow* or *life*. The resulting ambiguity was resolved by the addition of a silent sign called a determinative, to indicate the category of nouns to which the intended object belonged. Linguists term this decisive innovation, which also underlies puns today, the rebus principle.

Once Sumerians had hit upon this phonetic principle, they began to use it for much more than just writing abstract nouns. They employed it to write syllables or letters constituting grammatical endings. For instance, in English it's not obvious how to draw a picture of the common syllable *–tion*, but we could instead draw a picture illustrating the verb *shun*, which has the same pronunciation. Phonetically interpreted signs were also used to spell out longer words, as a series of pictures each depicting the sound of one syllable. That's as if an English speaker were to write the word *belief* as a picture of a bee followed by a picture of a leaf. Phonetic signs also permitted scribes to use the same pictorial sign for a set of related words, but to resolve the ambiguity with an additional phonetically interpreted sign.

Thus, Sumerian writing came to consists of a complex mixture of three types of signs: logograms, referring to a whole word or name; phonetic signs, used in effect for spelling syllables, letters, grammatical elements, or parts of words; and determinatives, which were not pronounced but were used to resolve ambiguities. Nevertheless, the phonetic signs in Sumerian writing fell far short of a complete syllabary or alphabet. Some Sumerian syllables lacked any written signs; the same sign could be pronounced in different ways; and the same sign could variously be read as a word, a syllable, or a letter.

Sumerian (Babylonian) cuneiform writing

Besides Sumerian cuneiform, the other certain instance of independent origins of writing in human history comes from Native American societies of Mesoamerica, probably southern Mexico. Mesoamerican writing is believed to have arisen independently of Old World writing, because there is no convincing evidence for pre-Norse contact of New World societies with Old World societies possessing writing. In addition, the forms of Mesoamerican writing signs were entirely different from those of any Old World script. About a dozen Mesoamerican scripts are known, all or most of them apparently related to each other, and most of them still only partially deciphered. At the moment, the earliest preserved Mesoamerican script is from the Zapotec area of southern Mexico around 600 B.C., but by far the best understood one is of the Lowland Maya region, where the oldest known written date corresponds to 292 A.D.

Despite its independent origins and distinctive sign forms, Maya writing is originated on principles basically similar to those of Sumerian writing and other western Eurasian writing systems that the Sumerian inspired. Like Sumerian, Maya writing used both logograms and phonetic signs. Logograms for abstract words were often derived by the rebus principle. That is, an abstract word was written with the sign for another word pronounced similarly but with a different meaning that could be readily depicted. Like the signs of Japan's kana and Mycenaean Greece's Linear B syllabaries, Maya phonetic signs were mostly signs for syllables of one consonant plus one vowel (such as *ta, te, ti, to, tu,*). Like letters of the early Semitic alphabet, Maya syllabic signs were derived from pictures of the object whose pronunciation began with that syllable (for example, the Maya syllabic sign "*ne*" resembles a tail, for which the Maya word is "*neb*").

All of these parallels between Mesoamerican and ancient western Eurasian writing testify to the underlying universality of human creativity. While Sumerian and Mesoamerican languages bear no special relation to each other among the world's languages, both raised similar basic issues in reducing them to writing. The solutions that Sumerians invented before 3,000 B.C. were reinvented, halfway around the world, by early Mesoamerican Indians before 600 B.C. (Diamond, J. 1997:215-264; Sacks, David 2003; Muley, Gunaker1972; Sahay, S.2000).

3. Other Writing Systems of the World

With the possible exceptions of the Egyptian, Chinese, Indus Valley and Easter Island writing to be considered later, all other writing systems devised anywhere in the world, at any time, appear to have been descendants of systems modified from or at least inspired by Sumerian or Egyptian or Indus Valley or Chinese or early Mesoamerican writing. One reason why there were so few independent origins of writing is the great difficulty of inventing it. The other reason is that other opportunities for the independent invention of writing were preempted by Sumerian or Indus Valley or Chinese or early Mesoamerican writing and their derivatives.

We know that the development of Sumerian writing took at least hundreds, possibly thousands, of years. Once the Sumerians and early Mexicans had invented writing, the details or principles of their writing spread rapidly to other societies, before they could go through the necessary centuries or millennia of independent experimentation with writing themselves. Similarly, Indus Valley Picto-phonographic script was invented in 2600 B.C. It took probably about 1,600 years to develop a Proto-Brahmi script (1000 B.C.); and then in turn took 200 years to develop South Indian Brahmi (800 B.C.) or North Indian Brahmi (800 B.C.). Thus, that potential for other, independent experiments was preempted or aborted (Diamond, J. 1997:215-264; Muley, Gunaker1972; Anderson, B. & Afonso, J.C. 1990).

4. Spread of writing systems in the world

The spread of writing has occurred by either of two contrasting methods, which find parallels throughout the history of technology and ideas. Someone invents something and puts it to use. Another then designs something similar for their own use, knowing that other people have already got their own model built and working. Such transmission of inventions assumes a whole spectrum of forms. At the one-end lies "**blueprint copying**", when you copy or modify an available detailed blueprint. Blueprint copying and modification of the existing script is the most straightforward option for transmitting technology. The other option is "**idea diffusion**", when one receives little more than the basic idea and has to reinvent the details. Knowing that it can be done, stimulates one to try and do it on his own and the eventual specific solution may not resemble that of the first inventor. The han'gul and ogham alphabets are examples of idea diffusion rather than to independent invention in isolation, because we know that both societies were in close contact with societies possessing writing.

The Roman alphabet itself was the end product of a long sequence of blueprint copying. Alphabets apparently arose only once in human history: among speakers of Semitic languages, in the area stretching from modern Syria to the Sinai, during the second millennium B.C. All of the hundreds of historical and now existing alphabets were ultimately derived from that ancestral Semitic alphabet, in a few cases (such as the Irish ogham alphabet) by idea diffusion, but in most by actual copying and modification of letterforms (Diamond, J. 1997:215-264).

5. The Evolution of Alphabet

The alphabet was invented in Egypt around 2,000 B.C. as a writing method to show sounds of words.

The alphabet was not the earliest writing: Egypt, Mesopotamia, China, and Indus Valley already had non-alphabetic systems of writing, but the alphabet was the most efficient writing system ever found, before or since. Like the wheel, it transformed the ancient world, and, like the wheel, it is still with us and has never been superseded. Today, about 4.8 billion

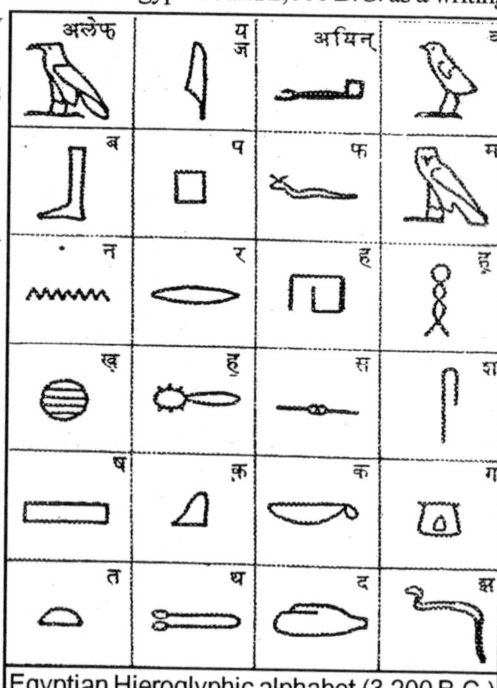

Egyptian Hieroglyphic alphabet (3,200 B.C.)

people, over three-quarters of humanity, live in countries that use an alphabet or a writing system modified from an alphabet.

THE PHOENICIAN ALPHABET OF 1000 B.C.

Letter Shape	Sound	Name	Name's Meaning	Descendant(s) in Our Alphabet
𐤀	breathing stop	*aleph*	ox	A
𐤁	"b"	*bayt*	house	B
𐤂	"g"	*gimel*	throwing stick	C
𐤃	"d"	*dalet*	door	D
𐤄	"h"	*he*	shout of surprise	E
𐤅	"w"	*waw*	peg	F, U, and Y
𐤆	"z"	*zayin*	ax	G and Z
𐤇	guttural "kh"	*khet*	fence	H
𐤈	emphatic "t"	*tet*	wheel	—
𐤉	"y"	*yod*	arm and hand	I
𐤊	"k"	*kaph*	palm of hand	K
𐤋	"l"	*lamed*	ox goad	L
𐤌	"m"	*mem*	water	M
𐤍	"n"	*nun*	fish	N
𐤎	"s"	*samek*	pillar	—
𐤏	guttural sound	*ayin*	eye	O
𐤐	"p"	*pe*	mouth	P
𐤑	"ts"	*tsade*	papyrus plants	—
𐤒	"q"	*qoph*	monkey	Q
𐤓	"r"	*resh*	head	R
𐤔	"sh"	*shin*	tooth	S
𐤕	"t"	*taw*	mark	T

The Egyptians never took the logical next step of discarding all their logograms, determinatives, and signs for pairs and trios of consonants, and using just their consonantal alphabet. Starting around 1700 B.C., though, Semites familiar with Egyptian hieroglyphs did begin to experiment with that logical step. Restricting signs to those for single consonants was only the first of three crucial innovations that distinguished alphabets from other writing systems. The second was to help users memorize the alphabet by placing the letters in a fixed sequence and giving them easy-to-remember names. The Semitic/ Phoenician names did possess meaning in Semitic languages: they were words for familiar objects. For instance, aleph = ox, beth=house, gimel= camel/ throwing sticks, daleth=door, and so on. These Semitic words were related "acrophonetically" to the Semitic consonants to which they refer: that is, the first letter of the word for the object was also the letter named for the object (a, b, g, d and so on). In addition, the earliest forms of the Semitic letters appear in many cases to have been pictures of those same objects. All these features made the forms, names, and sequence of Semitic alphabet letters easy to remember. Many modern alphabets retained, with minor modifications, the original sequence devised over 3,000 years ago. The third and last innovation leading to modern alphabets was to provide for vowels. Already in the early days of the Semitic alphabet, experiments had begun with methods for writing vowels by adding small extra letters to indicate selected vowels, or else by dots, lines, or hooks sprinkled over the consonantal letters. In the Eighth century B.C. the Greeks became the first people to indicate all vowels systematically by the same types of letters used for consonants. Greeks derived the forms of their vowel letters by co-opting five letters used in the Phoenician alphabet for consonantal sounds lacking in Greek.

Nearly every alphabet has been born from a prior alphabet. The letters have been copied from one language to another. Aside from the non-alphabetic writing systems of China and Japan, almost all major script in use today, anywhere in the world, belong to a single "alphabet family", stems entirely from the first Semitic-language-alphabet of 2000 B.C. This ancestor produced a prime descendant: the Phoenician or North Semitic alphabet, which, from its base in what is now Lebanon, became the launching pad for global proliferation. By 800 B.C., the convenient Semitic letters had been copied at least four times into other languages. Two of the resultant alphabets, the Aramaic and the Greek, spawned new alphabets in their own right, and these new alphabets, spawned still newer ones, in a steady progress east and west across the ancient world.

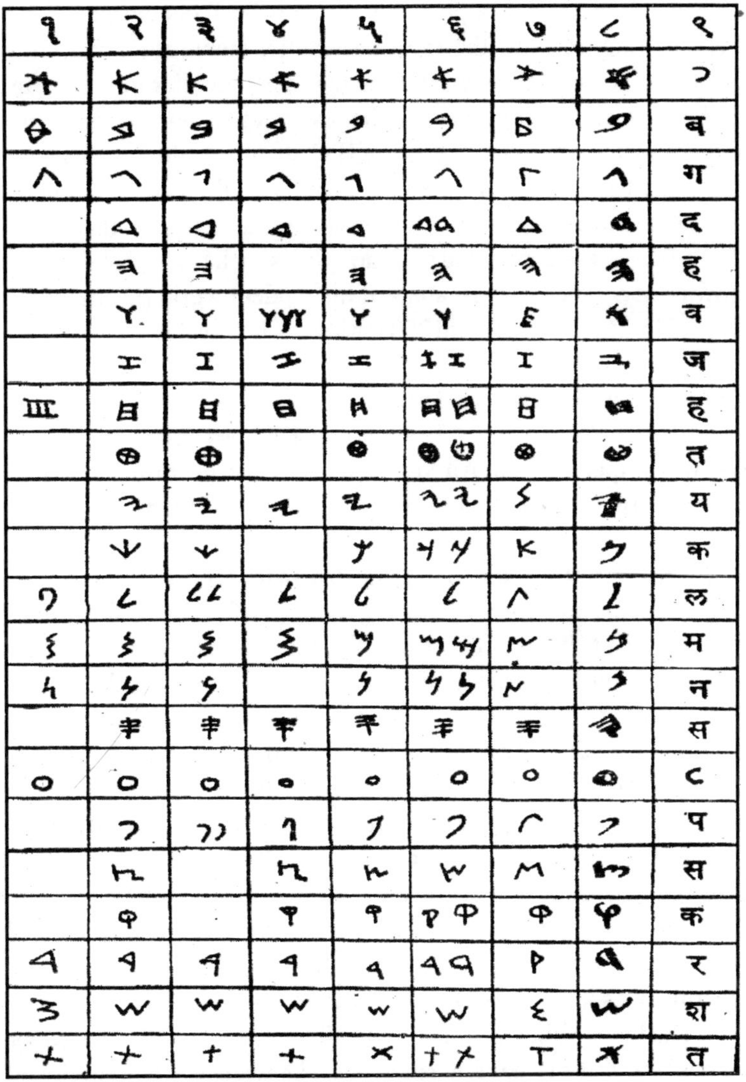

North Semitic Script (1800 -1500 B.C.)

Source: Muley G. 1972

From those earliest Semitic alphabets, one line of blueprint copying and evolutionary modification led via early Arabian alphabets to the modern Ethiopian alphabet. A far more important line evolved by way of the Aramaic alphabet, used for official documents of the Persian Empire, into the modern Arabic, Hebrew, Indian, and Southeast Asian alphabets. But the line most familiar to European and American readers is the one that led, via the Phoenicians to the Greeks by the early eighth century B.C., thence to the Etruscans in the same century, and in the next century to the Romans, whose alphabet with slight modifications is the one used to print this book. The advantage of combining precision with simplicity, alphabets have now been adopted in most areas of the modern world (Diamond, J. 1997:215-264; Sacks, David 2003; Muley, Gunaker1972).

6. Writing systems in India

Indus Valley scripts - Brahmi and Kharosti - are the earliest known scripts of India. Almost all regional scripts of India and its neighbouring countries were developed from the Brahmi script.

6.1 Indus Valley Picto-phonographic script

The earliest known writing system of India is the Indus Valley script. It has affinities with other ancient scripts, which extend from Easter Island in the east to Spain in the West. Historians and ethnologists believe that the Dravidians are a Mediterranean race and their original home was probably Libya. The people spread over the southern regions of Europe and Egypt in its pre-Dynastic days, were living in what seems to have been an important centre of culture in ancient times. Libyans brought this culture to India, and with time they came be known as Dravidians. They mixed with the Negritoes and Kolarians who were inhabiting India at the time and their culture was known as Dravidian Civilization.

The Indus Valley civilization (2,600 –1,700 B.C.) that lasted for about 1900 years is the civilization of the Dravidians. They developed a script known as Indus Valley Picto-phonographic script. Many seals have been discovered from excavations at the Mahenjo Daro and

Harappa sites. However, manuscripts written in this scripts have not yet found so far. Also, the script has not been deciphered fully as yet and thus, not much is known about the science behind it (Anderson, B. & Afonso, J.C. 1990:10-19; Muley, G. 1972: 167-170).

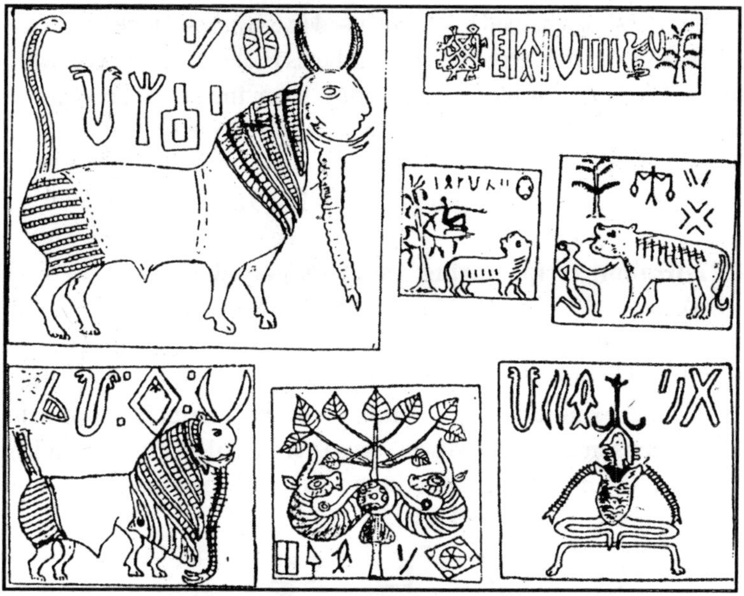

Indus Valley Script Seals (2,600 B.C.)

Source: Ibid

6.2 Brahmi Script

The Brahmi script of India is the parent of all the modern scripts of the subcontinent except Arabian and Kharosti script. Probably influenced by Phoenician or North Semitic alphabet, the people of India had developed a Proto-Brahmi script by 1000 B.C. from Indus Valley Picto-phonographic script. Based on this script South Indian Brahmi alphabet was developed by the Dravidians of South India by 800 B.C. Simultaneously, in the North India, the Aryans also developed the North Indian Brahmi alphabet from this proto-Brahmi script. Buddhist religious book "*Lalit-Vistar*" has mentioned 64 scripts, of which the first is Brahmi and the second Khoresti. Jain religious book "*Pannawonasutra*" and "*Samwayansutra*" have mentioned

16 scripts, of which, again, the first is Bambhi (Brahmi). In "*Bhagawatisutra*", the prayer starts with the prayer of Bambhi (Brahmi). "*Phawansulin*", a Chinese Buddhist Universal Dictionary written in 668 A.D. also mentions Brahmi and Kharosti scripts. The Emperor Ashoka named his script, used in the pillar/ stone/ rocks as *Dhomm* script. Indian mythology attributes Brahma, the creator, with the development of the Brahmi script. From the above account, it appears that Brahmi was an Indian script developed by the Indians in India. Brahmi is written from left to right (Muley, G. 1972: 167-170; Anderson, B. & Afonso J.C.1990: 10-19).

6.21 Brahmi script during Ashoka's period

Ashoka (272-232 B.C.) succeeded his father Bindusar in 272 B.C. and his coronation was held 4 years into his Kingṣhip (i.e. 269 B.C.), and he ruled for 37 years. He started religious writing after 12 years of being king (i.e. 257 B.C.). Ashoka's script had 6 vowels and 33 consonants and 6 vowel signs (i.e. aa, i, ii, e, ee), "·" (bindu) but no "nga", diphthong "uu", (both vowel and vowel sign) and half consonant sign (halanta) (Ibid:167-170).

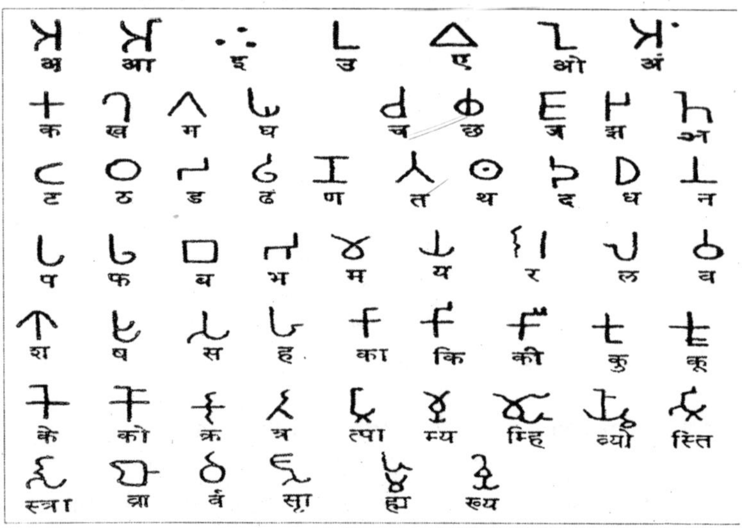

Brahmi script during Ashoka's time (272-232 B.C.)

Source: Muley G. 1972

6.22 Brahmi script upto the First Century A.D.

Some new letters were added in the alphabet by the first century: "ii" represented by four "bindus"; vowel-diphthongs such as "uu", "ai", "au" , "bri" ; ":" (bisargha) and half sounding r "ref" were introduced; the letters "gha", "bha", "la" and "sha" were written in a new style; a new letter "la" was also introduced. By this time Brahmi was also found written on coins. In South Indian Brahmi "da" facing left-side was modified to facing right-side as in the case of Devnagri (Ibid:167-170).

6.23 Brahmi script from the First to fourth century A.D.

The first difference of Brahmi script seen during this period was that the people had slowly started writing with pen. This has changed the styles of the letter in the northern India resulting thickness on the head-side of the letters. Secondly, "aa" vowel sign, which was a straight line on the right side has changed to curved on the upper side of the letter. Vowel signs of "i" and "ii" also became artistic rounded in form. The letters were compressed in height (i.e. ha, ya, madina, ma, cha etc.); some letters became triangular (i.e. wa, kha, and ma); some letters are beautifully lengthened and twisted; letter "ba" became larger and "tha" became artistic.; Vowel signs of "e" and "u" which were raised up towards left as well as right side (Ibid:167-170).

6.24 Brahmi script of the Gupta period (400 to 800 A.D)

During this period the Brahmi scripts were written with pens and the letters were of equal or more in width than height and more angular; more use of long sounding diphthongs; vowel signs started using a new method and more in length; sometimes letters were box-headed on the upper side; letter "om" was introduced, letter "nga" was introduced. The half-sounding consonant sign (halant) was introduced. The development of Brahmi script, which took place from 6th century to 8th century, is popularly known as "Kutil script". During this period, the Brahmi scripts were developing towards the Nagari or Nandinagari scripts. The shape of the upper part of the letters became rounded while the lower parts turned either towards left or right in Northern India. In southern India, the letters became rounded throughout. The Brahmi script development beyond 9th century A.D. is known as Prantiya Script. Almost all the prantiya scripts of India are developed from Brahmi. The early Prantiya scripts developed from Brahmi is without a line on the top of the letter while the prantiya scripts developed later are with a line on the top of the letter and look more like Devnagari (Diamond, J. 1997:215-264; Muley, Gunaker1972:168-210; Sahay, S.2000)

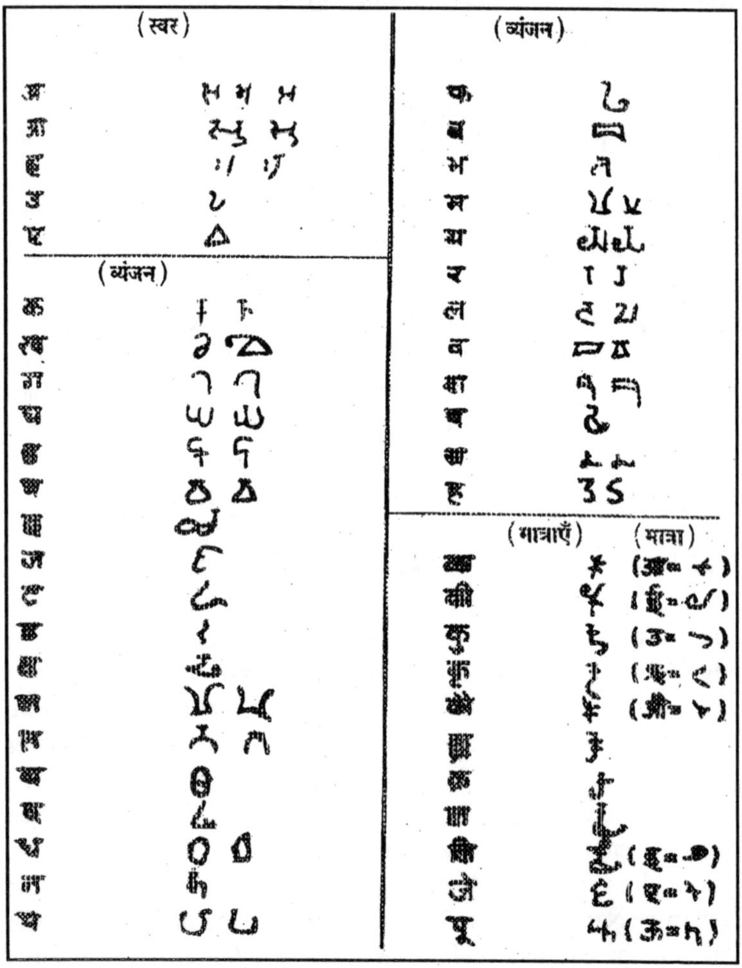

Brahmi script during Gupta's Period (400-800 A.D.)

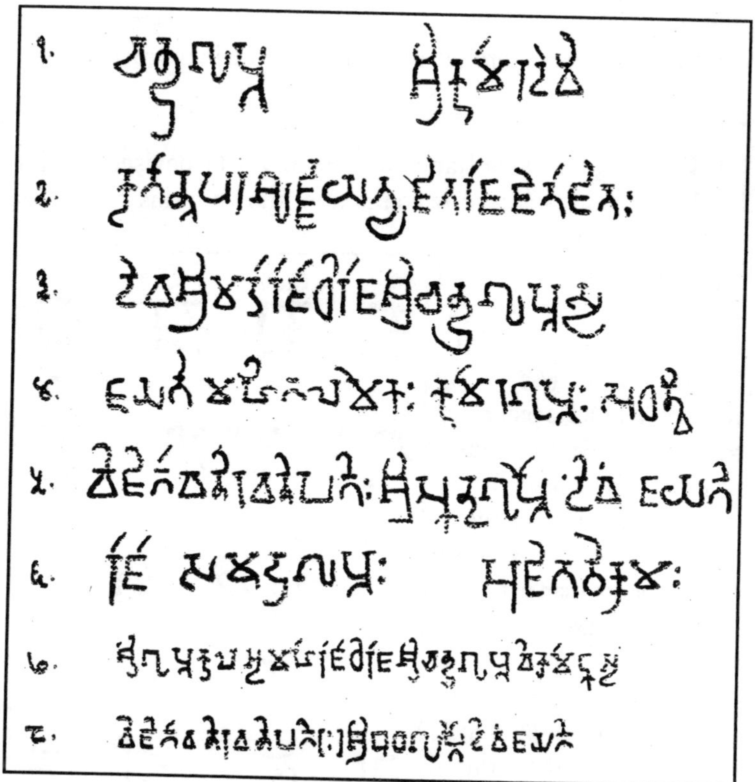

Gupta Period's Brahmi script on some coins (Ibid)

7. Writing systems in Sikkim

The Government of Sikkim has recognized eleven languages in Sikkim as the Official Languages of the State. These are Nepali (*Khas Kura*), Lepcha, Bhutia (Lhopo), Limboo, Magar, Tamang, Gurung, Khambu-Rai, Sunuwar, Sherpa, and English. Out of these, Nepali uses Devnagari script, Bhutia, Tamang, and Sherpa use Sambhota Tibetan script, while others have their own script developed for their languages by blueprint copying of Brahmi and other scripts developed from Brahmi. Today, professional linguists design writing systems for unwritten languages by resorting to blueprint copying. Most such tailor-made systems modify existing alphabets through some design syllabaries. Linguists of different communities of Sikkim have now designed writing systems for their unwritten languages through blueprint copying in the recent past.

7.1 Sirijunga script

The King Sirijunga Hang of 9th century A.D. devised a script for the Limboo language which is now known in his honour as "Sirijunga script".

He developed this script through blueprint copying of the Brahmi script of the Gupta period (4th to 8th century A. D.). He picked up some of the Brahmi letters which could be used for the Limboo language. Brahmi letters of this period were more in width than in height, hence, the width of the letters in Sirijunga script are more or equal to the height and without a line on the top as in the case of the Brahmi script of the Gupta period (unlike Devnagari script). Sirijunga selected only one main vowel letter "a". To pronounce different vowel sounds such as aa, i, u, e, o, e: and titcha, he added behind, above and below, various vowel-signs to the main vowel letter "a" to represent eight vowels (a, aa, i, u, e, o, e:, a-titcha). Thus, there are no independent vowel letters for i, u, e, ai, in the Srijunga script unlike Devnagari script. Sirijunga further selected out 19 consonant letters (ka, pa, ma, ta, ya, tha, na, sa, nya, sha, wa, ha, la, cha, pha, kha, ra, chha, and loo ("Om"), eight half-sounding letters (k, ny, n, t, p, r, l, m), two full-sounding sub-conjoint letters (ya, tra), three phonetic symbols (mukphrang, kemphremg, swai), and 10 digits (0 1 2 3 4 5 6 7 8 9).

Although we don't have any manuscript written by King Sirijunga himself with us today, but a copy of the scripts revived and popularized by his incarnate Sirijunga Teyongshi are available with the India Office Library, London. A photocopy set has been obtained from London and preserved in Archives of Sikkim. Blueprint copying of Gupta Brahmi script for the Limboo language contemporary to the development of Devnagari script in Northern India is the circumstantial evidence that supports the belief that the Sirijunga script was devised by King Sirijunga in the 9th Century. The letters of the Sirijunga Script are comparable to the Gupta Brahmi script. Later, Sirijunga Teyongshi (1704-1741) revived, propagated and popularized Sirijunga Hang's script.

Although, there was a tremendous influence of Devnagari script during Sirijunga Teyongshi's time, there was no addition or deletion of letters to the "Sirijunga script" during his period. However, during the period of Lalshore Sendang (1840-1926), and I. S. Chemjong (1904-1967), the influence of Nepali language, which was the lingua franca of the region by then, was tremendous. I.S.Chemjong was not fluent in Limboo language since he came from a Christian family, his father was priest in Kalimpong, West Bengal, and so he followed Lalshore Sendang and added many vowel and consonant letters directly from Devnagari script to the Sirijunga script. These additions are ii, uu (2 vowel diphthongs), ga, gha, anya, zdha, gya, da, dha, ba, bha, tra, zdha and gyan (12 consonant letters), and one half-sounding letter (sha) and one full-sounding letter (wa). Some problems always arise when an existing writing system is used as a blueprint for adoption by a different language because no two languages have exactly the same sets of sounds. Some inherited letters or signs may simply be dropped, when the sounds that those letters represent in the lending language do not exist in the borrowing language.

Thus, out of Chemjong's blueprint copying of Devnagari letters, only ii and uu (2 vowels), ga, gha, ba, bha, da (5 consonants), and wa (full-sounding sub-conjoint) are retained in the present day's Sirijunga script being used in Sikkim since B.B. Subba's (Muringla) appointment as Language resource person in 1975, and as a Limboo Language Textbook Writer in April, 1976. B.B.Subba (Muringla) and his associates Chandra Mangyung and Mohan Prasad Phurumbho became the team that streamlined the modern Sirijunga script and evolved an effective writing system of Limboo language in Sirijunga script. Now, the language is being taught upto University level

The modern Sirijunga script being used in Sikkim nowadays has 9 (nine) vowels (a, aa, i, u, e, ii, o, au, e:), 18 (eighteen) main consonants. Out of these consonants; 4 (four) are de-aspirates (ka, cha, ta, pa); 4 (four) aspirates (kha, chha, tha, pha); 4 (four) approximents (ya, ra, la, wa); 3 (three) fricative; and 3 (three) nasals (nga, na, ma). In Limboo language, the above vowel as well as consonant letters are essential to form a word, and hence known as the main letters. However, very few words are found from the main letters of "chha", "ra", and "sha". Other consonants are crafted when two or more words are compounded and these letters are known as helping consonants. They are 4 (four) de-aspirates (ga, ja, da, ba) and 3 (three) aspirates (gha, dha, bha). These letters originate by two different ways:

First, when the first word ends with small letters or nasals, "nga", "na", "ma" and the second word starts with ka, cha, ta, pa, kha, tha, pha, then the first letter of the second word ka, cha, ta, pa, kha, tha, pha in compound word becomes ga, ja, da, ba, gha, dha and bha respectively.

Second, any vowel compounding with ka, cha, ta, pa, kha, tha, pha becomes ga, ja, da, ba, gha, dha, and bha in the compound words.

In the beginning, when ga, ja, ba, gha, dha, bha were yet to develop, the main letters (ka, cha, ta, pa, kha, tha, pha) used to cater to the requirement of letters developed in the later stages: i.e. ka for ka and ga, kha for kha and gha, cha for cha and ja, chha for chha and jha, ta for ta and dha, tha for tha and dha, pa for pa and ba, and pha for pha and bha. However, jha is not pronounced in

Limboo language and hence kept pending for the time being. Thus, from the 18 (eighteen) main consonants, 7 (seven) helping consonants were added comprising a total of 25 consonants in the Limboo alphabets (Subba, B.B. 2004:110-116).

During the 19th and early 20th century, there was a tremendous influence of Nepali language in the entire Himalayan region of Nepal and Sikkim. This had a great influence on all the regional languages/dialects, including Limboo language of the region. Most probably this was the main reason why letters pronounced as *aa-karanta* (kaa, khaa, gaa, ghaa etc. like Tibetan alphabet) during the times of the two Sirijunga's upto 1741 A.D., were found being used as *a-karanta* in the early 20th century (1925 A.D.) by Lalshore Sendang, I. S. Chemjong and Bajbir Tholong in 1928-30 A.D. in their first booklet - "*Tumyakthung Ningwaphu Sapla*", along with the helping letters described above i.e. ga, ja, da, ba, gha dha and bha. We find a complete blueprint copying of Devnagari script in this booklet (Subba, J.R. 2002).

7.2 Devnagari or Nagari Script

Devnagari or Nagari script was developed through blueprint copying of later Gupta's Brahmi and Kutil scripts over the 8th and 9th century A.D. Nepali language (*Khas Kura*) is written in Devnagari or Nagari script, and this is the *lingua franca* of Sikkim today. Its speciality is the line on the top of each letter equal to the width of the letter. Manuscripts of Nagari script had started appearing from 9th century onwards in North India. Some manuscripts of this script were available in Southern India sometime before that (8th century) and was known as "Nandinagari". There is no unanimity on the place of origin and name. Some believe that the kings of Vijayanagar of South India used this script in their "*Danpatra*" and named it "Nandinagari", most probably after the name of Nandinagar (present Nander) where it was first used by the kings. The script is known interchangeably as "Nagari" or "Nandinagari".

Proto-Nagari form of Nagari script can be seen on the "*danpatra*" of King Sasanka of West Bengal. King Sasanka was contemporary of Harsa Vardhan. King Mahendrapal (891-907

A.D.) of Pratihar dynasty was the first to use Nagari script in his "*Danpastra*" in Northern India. In this script, the letters are more in height than in length, and have a line on the top of the letters. After that, a number of manuscript are available in this script in Northern India. These are "*Danpatras*"of Guhil dynasty, Chahman dynasty, Rastrakut, Chalukya, Paramroh, Chandel dynasty, Haheya etc. of North Indian Kings; Pallavi administrators, Pandaya administrators of 8th century, Pandaya king of Bargun of 9th century of South India. Kings Rajraj and Rajendra of Cholla dynasty used this script for the first time in their coins (Muley, Gunaker 1972: 216-219).

There are 11 vowels, 10 vowel signs, and 33 consonants. Besides, the script also has signs such as Chandrabindu, Sirbindu and Bisargha (Sharma, Purnima in Lipi Sangalo (ed) by Limboo, R.B. 1998:19-28).

7.3 Sambhota Script of Bhutias, Sherpas and Tamangs

The Bhutia or Lhopo or Lhokey language is written in Sambhota Script, and taught upto the University level in Sikkim. The Sherpa and Tamang languages are also written in Sambhota script and taught up to the primary level of education since their recognition as official languages in Sikkim in 1997.

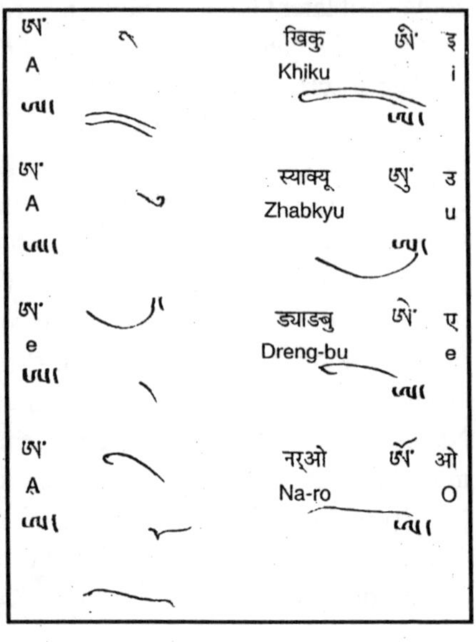

Before 7th century A.D. the people of Tibetan region were nomads - hunter-gatherers, divided under a number of leaders. Tibetan people were still nomads when Hiuen Tsang, a Chinese pilgrim, visited India during the reign of Harsa Vardhan of North India. Srang-Tsen Gampo, born in 629 A.D. in the valley of Shangpo river known as Lhokha, consolidated the leaders of the nomad hunter-gatherers of Tibet and established a kingdom extending from Kashmir in the west to the China in the east. He established a capital, named first as Rasa (*Ajbhumi*) and later renamed Lhasa (*Devbhumi*). He was so powerful that king Amsu Varman of Thakur Dynasty, who ruled Nepal from 635 to 650 A.D., gave his daughter Bhrikuti in marriage to him. Similarly, the emperor of China got his daughter Kongjyo married to Srang-Tsen Gampo. The Chinese queen brought a book on Buddhism with her. The king constructed a Gompa for his queens, and thus began Buddhism in Tibet.

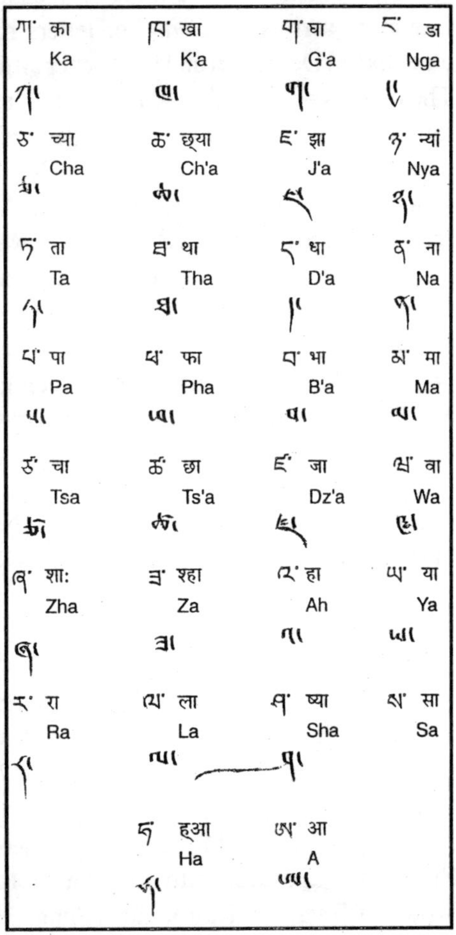

Now, the king was in need of a script for administration. He deputed one of his Ministers – Sambhota of Thonmi area for the task.

Tradition holds that Thonmi Sambhota came to India to study Indian scripts, but there is no evidence to support this belief. During that time, the people of Tungut/Tarim region of northern Tibet were aware of the Indian script and Buddhism. Hence, it appears that Sambhota developed the Tibetan script through blueprint copying of Indian Gupta Brahmi script already being used extensively by the people of Tungut/Tarim region of Northern Tibet (Muley, Gunaker

1972: 235-237). Rahul Sankrityanan (1956-57) believes that Sambhota developed the Tibetan script from the contemporary North Indian Gupta Brahmi script, which was also popular in the Mid-Asian region.

The Tibetan language falls under the Tibeto-Burman family. Thus pronunciation of six letters – gha, jha, arda, achha, bha and Mardisa do not have sounds in Tibetan language. Hence, Sambhota left these letters out. However, there are cha, chha, jha, sa incorporated but pronounced differently in Tibetan language. Therefore, he codified separate letters for these letters. Tibetan letters are of two types: Literature scripts "*U-Chan*" or letters having lines on top of the letter like in Devnagari and look better an are used for printing books. The other types called "*U-Med*" or the letters without a line on the top of the letters, used for day-to-day writing. Rahul Sankrityanan opined that the latter script was developed from the Gupta Brahmi script available with the people of Tungut/ Tarim region. In the Tibetan script, there are four vowels: e, u, a, o which are short pronounced equal to one and half, 30 consonants equal to one and half length. Sambhota also wrote a Tibetan grammar for Tibetan language (Muley, Gunaker 1972: 235-237).

In Sikkim, Sambhota script is being used for Bhutia, Sherpa and Tamang languages with little or no modifications. The preferred names for the script here are "Lhokey script" for Bhutia, "Sambhota" script for Sherpa, and "Tamayek" script for Tamang. (Chichhudarpo, Bhaichung, Dawa Gyatso Sherpa, and K.M. Tamang in Lipi Sangalo (ed) by Limboo R.B. 1998:10-16; 90-112).

7.4 Lepcha Script

Lepcha language is written in Lepcha script in Sikkim and West Bengal. One school of belief has it that the Lepcha alphabet, known as "Rong Chhyo", was developed by Maw Rong Hang, a powerful Buddhist King of Eastern Nepal in the 7th century A.D. probably by blueprint copying of the Gupta's Brahmi script for his Lepcha subjects. Being a Buddhist king, Maw Rong Hang translated many Buddhist scriptures into Lepcha or Rong language. Karthak Wookdey Sung, the Timi Kanden Sung, the Lingebu Sung, the Guru

Chhyo Ong Namthar, the Tasey Sung Namthar and Nangshe Sung Namthar are Lepcha translations of Tibetan literature. Almost ten percent of the Tibetan language was amalgamated in the Lepcha language. Although king Maw Rong Hang preached and practiced Buddhism to his subjects, he did not discourage them from following their own cultures (Chenjong, I. S. 1967/2003 ed.: 94). Thus, the Lepchas had a literary tradition extant before the arrival of Buddhism in Sikkim.

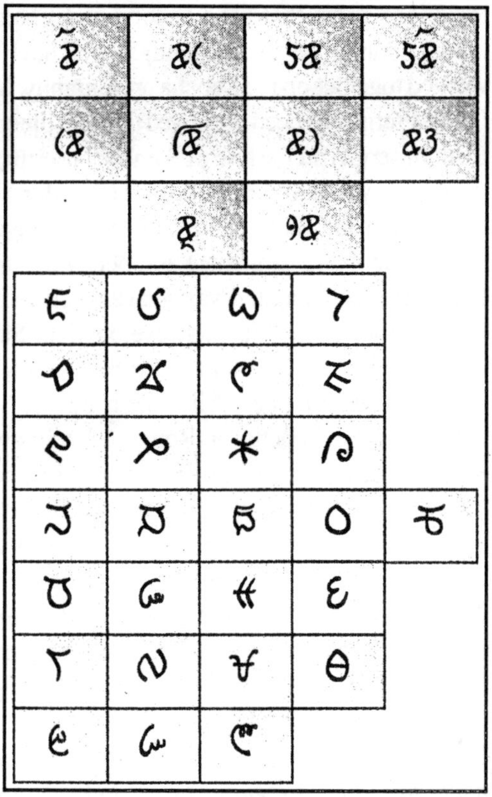

It however seems more likely that the need for a Lepcha script was motivated by the religious activities of Buddhist missionaries in these parts. The Buddhist monks were keen to communicate with the Lepcha people in their own language, and as so often happens when the influence of a new religion spreads, religious texts were translated into the local language of the area, in this case Lepcha, for which an alphabet was created. There are many who believe that there was no writing system amongst the Lepchas when Bhutias established the Chiefdom in Sikkim in 1642 A.D. and the that third Chogyal Chagdor Namgyal developed the Lepcha script (Plaisier 2003: 20-23, Risley 1894: 13, Sprigg 1983, 1996). I personally do not subscribe to this view since it is incomprehensibe for me how the aboriginal

Lepchas could have not developed a script till the end of 18th century when their contemporary Limboo tribes had their own script since the 9th century A,D.

The others view is that ofthe Lepcha tradition, the native Lepcha orthography was created by Lepcha scholar Thikung Mon Solong, who is believed to have been a contemporary of Lama Lhatsun Namkha Jigme (1597-1654), who arrieved in Sikkim in 1646 A.D. and played a definitive part in Sikkim's conversion to Buddhism. Since local lore states that Mon Solong and Lhatsun Chempo met each other (Foning 1987: 152), it might well have been the case that they worked together on the Lepcha orthography. Most likely, the existing Lepcha script has been improved through blueprint copying of Gupta's Brahmi script (on the line of Sambhota script) during the reign of the third Chogyal of Sikkim, Chogyal Chagdor Namgyal (1700-1716 A. D.). He was in Lhasa for several years, studying hard, and gradually rose to scholastic eminence and became Chi-Tung-yig to the Dalai Lama. Hence, Chagdor Namgyal as well as Lhatsun Chempo knew how, Thonmi Sambhota had developed the Sambhota script from the Gupta Brahmi script. Whatsoever be the fact, let the Lepcha scholars do more research to establish the truth.

Thus, the Lepcha or Rong script known as *Mutanchi Rong Aming* developed during 7th or early 18th century has ten vowels (*Aa-Kup Amingpong*) – *a, aa, ae, ai, ao, aoo, au, auo, aey, aong*; ten conjoint vowels (*mingtalpong*) *a-kup, aa-kup, ae-kup, ai-kup, ao-kup, aoo-kup, au-kup, auo-kup, aey-kup, ang-kup*; 28 consonants (*Amoo Amingping*) – *ka, kha, ga, nga, chya, jya, nya, ta, tha, da, na, pa, pha, pa, ba, ma, tsa, tsha, za, ya, ra, la, ha, va, sya, sa, wa* (as in the case of Devnagri); 8 conjoint letters (*Mingtalpeng*) - *ka-kup, ma-kup, ra-kup, pa-kup, ta-kup, nga-kup, na-kup, la-kup*; and Numbers (*Fron-kheyop*) – *tee, kat, nget, sam, flee, fongugu, tarok, kukyok, kukua* (Lepcha, A.T. in Lipi Sangalo (ed) by Limboo, R.B. 1998: 17-20).

7.5 Ranjana and Prachalit Scripts of Newars

The Newar language is written in Ranjana and Prachalit script and taught upto primary level in the schools of Sikkim since its

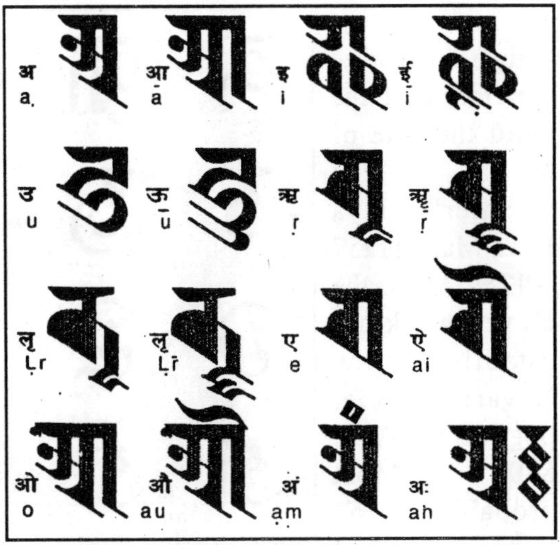

recognition as one of the official languages of the State in 1997. The Ranjana script is used in decorative and religious texts, while Prachalit is used in day to day and school texts in Sikkim and Nepal. Most probably, the Ranjana script has also been developed by blueprint copying of Gupta's Brahmi script sometime in the 13th century (Malla period) in Nepal. Verma Deva (1083 –1093 A.D.) was the founder of second Thakur Dynasty of Amsu Varman, which gave twelve kings. Sadasiva Deva, the third king of this line, built Kirtipur on a hill south-west of Kathmandu. He introduced copper coins alloyed with iron, marked with the figure of a lion. Ari Deva (1224 – 1257 A.D.), the ninth king, was wrestling when he received word that

a son had been born to him, and he therefore gave the child the title of Malla "the wrestler". Jaya Deva Malla (1257 – 1286 A.D.), the eleventh king, established the Nevari era, beginning A.D. 880. Most probably, the Ranjana script of Nevar or Newar was developed during the reign of Jaya Deva Malla from the Brahmi and Kutil scripts of Gupta's period. He ruled over Lalitapattana whilst his younger brother Ananda Malla founded Bhaktapura or Bhatgaon and ruled there. The era of second Thakur Dynasty of Amsu Varman ends with the last king Ananda Malla who reigned from 1286 to 1302 A.D (Vansittart, E. 1896: 15).

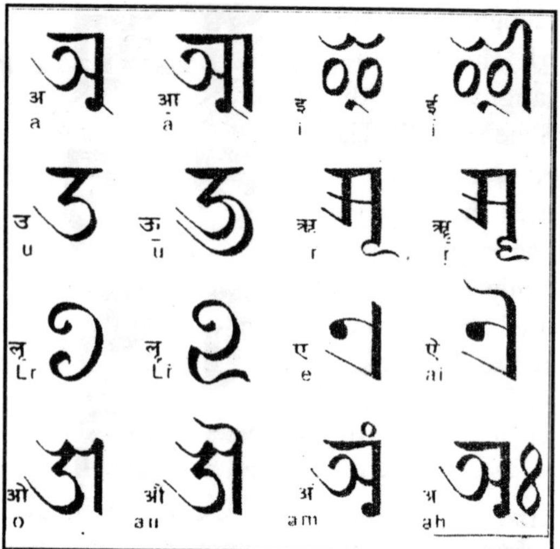

The Prachalit script was developed later from Ranjana as it is easier for day to day writing system during the Malla period. The scripts were greatly influenced by Devnagari script which was popular in Northern India during those time, which is evident from the alphabets, which differs only slightly in form of the letters.

The script has 16 vowels – a, aa, i, ii, u, uu, r, rr, lr, lrr, e, ai, o, au, am, and ah; 36 consonants – ka, kha, ga, na, ca, cha, ja, jha, nya, ta, tha, da, dha, na, pa, pha, ba, bha, ma, ya, ra, la, va, sha, sa, sa, ha, aksa, tra, and ghyan (Pradhan, G. K. in Lipi Sangalo (ed) by Limboo, R.B. 1998: 41-53).

7.6 Sunuwar Script (Koinch Bress):

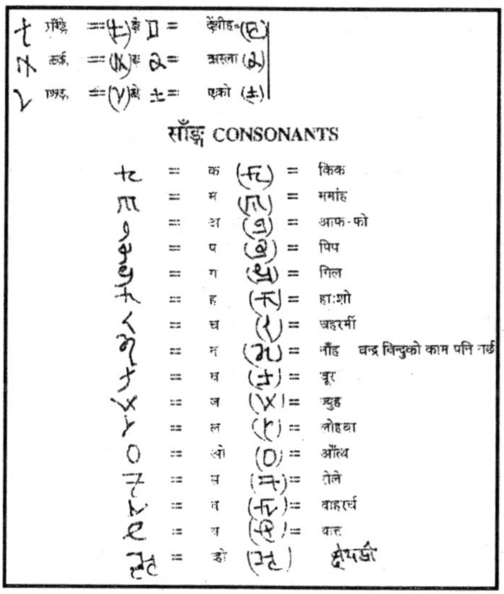

The Sunuwar language is written in Sunuwar script known as "Koinch Bress" or "Koinch Bnu" since its recognition as one of the official languages of Sikkim in 1997. Now, it is being taught upto primary level in the schools of Sikkim. The Sunuwars believe that Karna Bahadur Jehntich, an Army Officer engaged in army signals developed the script combining wireless signals and Brahmi script in the 19th century. The script has three vowels and 16 consonants. A considerable effort is yet to be put in for further development of writing systems in this script (personal interview with many Sunuwars; Mukhia, R.B. in Lipi Sangalo (ed) by Limboo, R.B. 1998: 113-139)

7.7 Akkha or Akkharika Script of Magars:

The Magar language is written in Akkha script and is being taught in the schools upto the primary level in Sikkim since its recognition as one of the official languages of the State in 1997. The script seems to have been developed from the early Brahmi script since the form of the letters is the same as that of the first to fourth century Brahmi. Most probably, the script was developed in the 11th century during the reign of Mukunda Sen (1100 A.D.), a powerful Magar king of Palpa and Botwal, who invaded Nepal Valley with a large number of mounted troops and subdued Hari Deva, the son of Rama Singha Deva , the last king of Karnataki Dynasty of Nepal. The principal seat of the Magars covered most of the central and lower parts of the mountains between the Jingruk (Rapti of Gorakhpur) and Marsiangdi rivers. They have resided in Palpa since time immemorial. However, there is no mention of any Magar script being developed and propagated by any of the Magar kings of Palpa and Botwal in any historical records (Vansittart E.1896: 17). Perhaps, owing to the geographical position of the tract of the country inhabited by the Magars, they were the first to receive immigrants from the plains of India and thus they never felt necessity to develop or propagate their own Akkha script. However, it is yet to be ascertained who, where and when the script was developed.

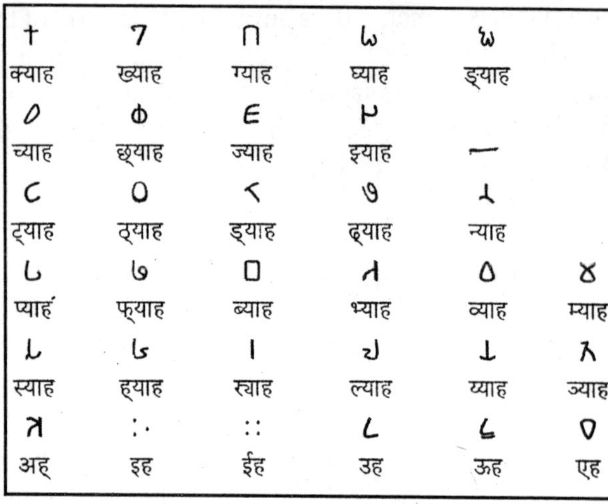

The script has 6 vowels (a, i, ii, u, uu, eh), 6 Semi-vowels (syha, hayha, syha, lyha, yyha, nyha), 10 vowel signs (aa, e, ee, u, uu, i, ii, o, oo, a:) and 20 consonants - 5 Velar (kyah, khayha, gyaha, ghyaha, nyaha), 4 Palatal (chyaha, chhyaha, dzyaha, yaha),

5 Retroflex (ttyaha, thyaha, dhyaha, dhhyaha, nyaha), and 6 Bi-labial (pyaha, phyaha, byaha, bhyaha, bbyaha, myaha) (Alle, Santosh, 2003:170-179; Thapa, Y.B. in Lipi Sangalo (ed) by Limboo, R.B. 1998:69-89).

7.8 Khema Script of Gurungs:

The Gurung language is written in Khema script and taught in the schools up to the primary level of education since the recognition of Gurung language as one of the official languages of Sikkim in 1997. It is yet to be ascertained who, where and when the Khema script was developed. A majority of Gurung experts suggest that the script was developed in Nepal from the Sambhota Tibetan script, but looking at the form of the letters, the script has strong influences of both, the Devnagari and Sambhota Tibetan scripts. In any case, the script was perhaps developed based on Brahmi script after the development of Sambhota and Devnagari scripts. The Khema script has the characters of both Sambhota and Devnagari scripts.

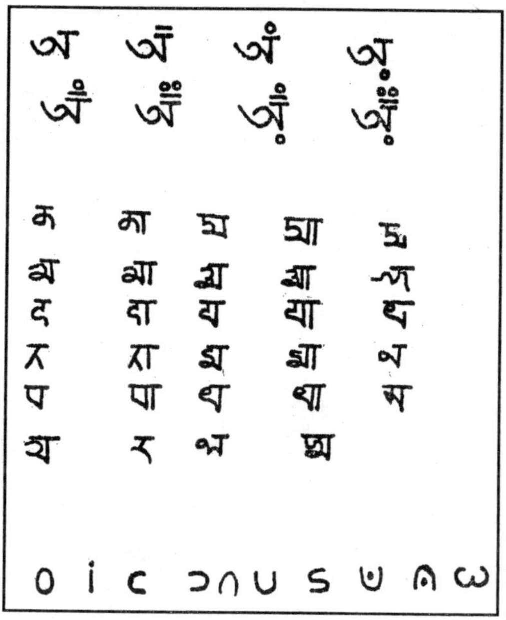

The Khema script of Gurungs has 7 vowels (a, e, u, i, ii, o, au), 7 vowel signs (aa, e, u, i, ii, o, au) and 29 consonants (same as Devnagari post-fixed with "khe"). The alphabets are the same as those of Devnagari but the vowels are read with post-fixed "ma" while the consonants post-fixed with "khe" (Gurung, Meghraj in Lipi Sangalo (ed) by Limboo, R.B.1998: 63-68).

7.09 Rai Script of Khambu-Rai:

The Khambu-Rai languages of 38 sub-tribes is written in Khambu-Rai script developed by Late Kripasalyan Rai in 1981-82 from the Devnagari script. The Khambu-Rai language (Bantawa language) is taught in schools up to the primary level ever since the Khambu-Rai language was recognized as one of the official languages of Sikkim in 1997.

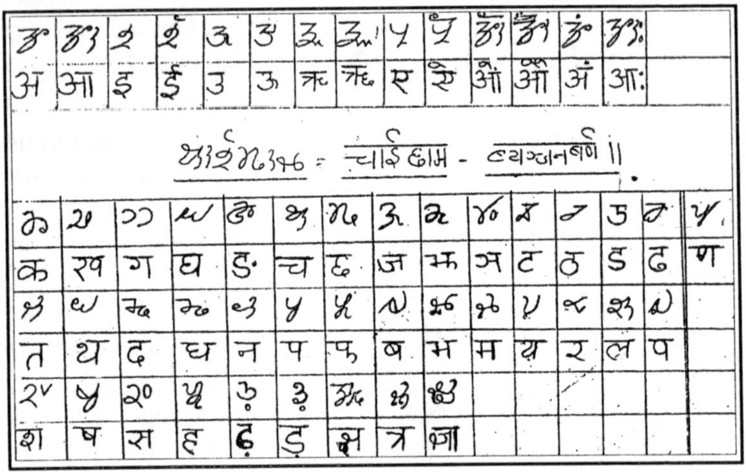

The Khambu-Rai script has the same letters as that of Devnagari with 14 vowels, 13 vowel signs, and 38 consonants (Rai, Krishnadas in Lipi Sangalo (ed) by Limboo, R.B. 1998:54-59).

4
The Evolution of Modern Society

Pre-history, properly speaking, is outside the field of history. History is the written exposition of the result of the search for facts about people of the past. One may find a bone or crude drawings on cave walls or ceilings, perhaps some remnants of buildings or fragments of statues, but these relics do not tell us who were the authors of that primitive civilization. These remains, for example, do not tell us what language the people spoke, what race they belonged to, what social life they lived, what religion they professed, and what were the relations they had with other similar beings. Evidently the account that may be written after the study of those pre-historic relics cannot be reasonably systematic because there is no cohesion amongst them. These missing agglutinant elements would come from written records from that time only, but these, unfortunately, are unknown to pre-history.

In the Indian context, when the Indus Valley civilization had not yet been discovered, some strict writers might have started the historic period of India from the middle of the so-called Vedic period, excluding the Rigvedic times from it. This, because the Rigveda was not a written document. But the Indus Valley discoveries completely changed the situation and carried back the beginning of history of India to many centuries earlier. The most striking discovery of the Indus Valley is the collection of inscribed seals, the importance of which lies precisely in the fact that they are historical documents. Thus, the pre-historic period of India ends with the appearance of the culture of the Indus Valley, which marks the first steps of historical man in India; while the proto-historic period would embrace the culture of the proto-Indians proper, that is Indus Valley people, the so-called Vedic period and the age of the Epics (Hiras, H. 1942:113-120).

1. Proto-historic people of India:

Not much is known about the proto-historic people of India. Migration of Dravidians from the Mediterranean area to India is also not established with much certainty. However, the culture of Indus Valley as illustrated from the ancient Sanskrit literature and inscriptions of Mohenjo Daro and Harappa, reveals that the Indus Valley civilization was the civilization of Dravidians, who were there in India before the Aryas. Rigveda itself speaks of the fight between the Aryas and the Dasyus from the moment they crossed the Hindu Kush-Himalayas. During the epic period, numerous Dravidians still inhabited Northern India. References to the Gandharas, the Mahisis, the Matsyas, the Nagas, the Garudas, and Bahlikas, point to the presence of much Dravidian blood in the veins of North-Indian people. Brahui and Uraon, two Dravidian languages now spoken in Northern India, also suggest the domination of the ancient Dravidians over the whole of North India. Historians and ethnologists opine that the Dravidians formed a part of the great Mediterranean race. Their original home was probably Libya, whose people spread over the southern countries of Europe and Egypt in its pre-dynastic days, and which seems to have been an important centre of culture in ancient times. Libyans, who were later called Dravidians, brought this culture to India, and it improved with their mixture with the Negritoes and Kolarians who inhabited India at the time of their arrival.

The name of India at the time of the glory of Mohenjo Daro was "Sid", which means stream, "to flow", in Dravidian languages. At a later period, the nasal "n" was added to it and finally the "u" was suffixed, becoming "Sindu" which was the form that the word had at the time of the Aryan arrivals.

The inscriptions of Mohenjo Daro unearthed so far speak of four great divisions called countries and its ancient people into which "Sid" was parceled, viz., Minad or the country of Fish; Paravanad or the country of Birds; Marankotinad or the country of the

Woodpecker; and Elnad or the Seven Countries (Heras, H. 1942;113-120).

The country and the ancient people are:

(i) Minad

This was the country of the Minas and was the largest and most important of all the four countries. This country extended from North to the south India. The people were strong, enterprising and prosperous. There occupations were fishing and trade. Some Minas were owners of land. They had comfortable and well-built houses. Their original totem was the unicorn, which is the most common animal in the seals discovered, but the symbol on their flag was of Two Fishes. The Minas lived in what is now Western Sind on the right bank of the Indus and along its lower course. When the Aryas invaded India, they were still there. Two cities of this country are specially mentioned – Nandur and Udayur. Udayur originally belonged to the tribe of the Bilavas – archers and hunters by profession. Their descendants are the Bhils and perhaps the Veddas of Ceylon. But they were also tilling the soil and were good cultivators. A section of this tribe were called Velvel Bilavas. They used to worship five tridents. Some Bilavas were not living in cities, but in caves. They worshipped the linga or phallus. Another section of Bilavas was Eruvus, who were busy in the gold mines of Northern India. Another tribe called Etkalis, "the spiders", were weavers, and not in friendly relations with the Bilavas. There was another tribe called Kavals. They were robbers. The Kavals united with another tribe the Kalakilas, "united leaves", who are often mentioned in Puranic literature as Kilakilas or Kilakalas. Some of them were merchants.

(ii) Paravanad

This country was the country of the Paravas (birds). They are still numerous on the Coromandel coast in South India and in Srilanka. The Paravas were a section of the Minas. There were two subdivsions of the Paravas: Pagal Paravas and Nile Paravas, i.e. Sun Paravas and Moon Paravas. The Moon Paravas seem to have been the more important of the two, and constituted one fourth of the whole Mina stock. Their occupations were fishing, as the rest of the Minas, trade and agriculture. They had also coconut plantations.

(iii) Marankotinad

This country was called the Middle country, which perhaps are meant to be the range of the Himalayas and the Hindu Kush. This would place the country of the woodpecker in the northernmost regions of India. The people of the country were Velalirs or Velalas, who are still numerous in South India. They exercised trade and successfully tilled the land. They worshipped the trident and linga.

(iv) Elnad

This country, which means the seven countries, is not mentioned too often in the inscriptions. Coconut plantations existed in it. Besides the above information about persons and places, several other tribes also find mention in the inscriptions of Mohenjo Daro. These are:

Alinas (Squirrels): a tribe mentioned in the Rigveda as having fought against Sudas in the battle of the ten kings.

Kolis (Fowls): they are still in the neighborhood of Mumbai and other places in Western India.

Munkalir (three-legged people):

Nagas (Serpents): Very frequently mentioned in Puranic literature. They believed in spirits and demons.

Nalakir (People that rise high): They are said to lead a happy life.

Nalkalir (Four-legged people): They were agriculturists.

Pareanir (Drum-players): It is the word corresponding to the name of the present Pariahs, though there is no foundation for identifying the social status of these groups of people (ibid:113-120).

1.1 Migration of Aryans to India

Proto-Indian Indus Valley seals of Mohenjo Daro and Harappa discovered in Ur or in other places of ancient Sumer reveal that a few merchants from Indus Valley seem to have found their way to

Mesopotamia. The Indian merchants going to Mesopotamia, Kingdom of Baberu (Babylon), were attracted to a crow unknown to them and bringing on board the ship with them a crow at 100 piece of money, and in turn selling Indian peacocks to the merchants of Baberu at 1000 piece of money is evident from a Buddhist story of the ancient times. As per the Rigveda, these merchants were the Dravidian Panis, people who never give anything, not even to the priests for the sacrifices.

The leaders of the Aryas, the Asura, Indar – called afterwards in the Vedic hymns Indra, did not dare to take the whole nation to the new land first. First they wanted to make a trial. They took two families with them, the families of Yadus and Turvasas, and embarking in one of the ships of the Panis, they set sail from lower Mesopotamia and after a number of days landed on the shores of Kathiawar (Saurastra in ancient times). This first expedition of the Aryas into India across the ocean is mentioned several times in the Rigveda. When the Yadus and the Turvasas were definitely settled in the country in friendship with, and with the acquiescence, of the Dravidian rulers, Indar, their valiant leader, returned at Assyria on a Pani vessel and started to prepare to exodus of the whole Aryan nation. It was then that Vrthra, probably an Assyrian monarch, was slain by the hero of the Aryas, and by his means also the whole of the country was flooded, a flood which saved the Aryas from the fury of the Assyrian army after the death of their monarch. Finally Indar could take away the Aryan nation to the country of the Sun (India) by land. But they encountered numerous enemies on their way, they fought innumerable battles and surmounted innumerable perils. In the midst of all these troubles they remained leaderless and helpless, when Indar himself perished perhaps in the fray of a battle in Turkestan. The first effect of Indar's death was inaction in the Aryan nation, surrounded by enemies and in an unknown country. That is the reason why the Iranian sources place their homeland across the Oxus, viz, not their original homeland which was already forgotten, but the homeland where they settled, undoubtedly for years, before their final incursion into Iran. The second effect was the split in the Aryan nation immediately caused by the deification of Indar. A section of the Aryan nation, under the influence of a religious preacher, who was probably Zaratustra himself, could not agree to the deification of a simple man, and as the effect of a natural reaction placed Indra's name amongst the names of demons.

The other section having finally found a new leader, probably Divodasa, and thence continued their march towards the country of the Sun (India). When they finally crossed its boundaries and settled in Saptasindhu first and then in Madhyadesa, they tried to effect a union with the Yadus and the Turvasas settled on the western coast. "May we see Turvasa and Yadu" prays Devatithi in one of the Rigvedic hymns.

Once the union was effected, the Yadus and the Turvasas learned of the death of their leader and of his consequent deification. Then they raised a temple to Indar on the place where he landed on the Suarastra shores, when they had arrived in their new country. Later, when the devotion to Indra dwindled after the death of those who had known him personally and subsequently to the amalgamation of Aryan and Dravidian deities and tenets, the ancient worship of the linga of Siva at Prabhaspatan became popular once again, as a referrence to it in the Agni Purana proves. Thus, the arrival of Aryans in India marked the beginning of the Aryan culture in India (Heras, H. in Andeson, B. and Afonso, J.C. 1990 eds: 44-86).

2. Socio-Anthropological Categories of Societies

Cultural anthropologists, in their attempt to describe the diversity of human societies, often divide them into as many as half a dozen categories. Any such attempt to define stages of any evolutionary or developmental continuum is doomed to imperfection. First, because each stage grows out of some previous stage, the lines of demarcation are inevitably arbitrary. Second, developmental sequences are not invariant, so examples pigeonholed under the same stage are inevitably heterogeneous. Nevertheless, arbitrary delineated stages provide useful shorthand for discussing the diversity of human societies, provided one bears in mind the above caveats. With that spirit, a simple classification based on just four categories: band, tribe, chiefdom, and state has been popularly adopted to understand the evolution of the modern societies (Diamond, J.1997: 267-268).

Types of Societies

	Band	*Tribe*	*Chiefdom*	*State*
Membership:				
Number of people:	dozens	hundreds	thousands	over 50,000
Settlement pattern:	nomadic	fixed: 1 village villages	fixed: 1 or more villages	fixed: many
Basis of rela- -tionships:	kin	kin-based clans	class and residence	class and residence
Ethnicities and languages	1	1	1 or more	1 or more
Government:				
Decision-making leadership:	egalitarian	egalitarian or big-man	centralized, hereditary	centralized
Bureaucracy:	none	none	none or 1 or 2 levels	many levels
Monopoly of force and information:	no	no	yes	yes
Conflict resolution:	informal	informal	centralized	laws, judges
Hierarchy of settlements:	no	no	no to para- mount village	capital
Religion:				
Justifies kleptocracy:	no	no	yes	yes to no

	Band	*Tribe*	*Chiefdom*	*State*
Economy:				
Food production:	no	no to yes	yes to intensive	intensive
Division of labour:	no	no	no to yes	yes
Exchanges: redistributive	reciprocal	reciprocal	redistributive (tribute)	(taxes)
Control of land:	band	clan	chief	various
Society:				
Stratified:	no	no	yes, by kin	yes, not by kin
Slavery :	no	no	small-scale	large-scale
Luxury goods for elite:	no	no	yes	yes
Public architecture:	no	no	no to yes	yes
Indigenous literacy:	no	no	no to yes	often

Source: (Diamond, J.1997: 268-269).

2.1 People in Sikkim under Band Social Status (? -700A.D.)

They are the tiniest societies, consisting typically of 5 to 80 people, most or all of them close relatives by birth or by marriage.

In fact, a band is an extended family or several related extended families. Today, bands still living autonomously are almost confined to the most remote parts of New Guinea and Amazonia, but in modern times many others have only recently fallen under state control or have been assimilated or exterminated. These include many or most African Pygmies, southern African San hunter-gatherers (Bushmen), Aboriginal Australians, Eskimos (Inuit), and Indians of some resource-poor areas of the Americas such as Tierra del Fuego and the northern boreal forests. All these modern bands are or were nomadic hunter-gatherers rather than settled food producers.

Probably all humans lived in bands until at least 40,000 years ago, and most still did till as recently as 11,000 years ago. Our closest animal relatives, the gorillas and chimpanzees and bonobos of Africa, also live in bands. All humans presumably did so too, until improved technology for extracting food allowed some hunter-gatherers to settle in permanent dwellings in resource-rich areas and grow larger. The band is the political, economic, and social organization that we inherited from our millions of years of evolutionary history. Our developments beyond it, took place in the last few tens of thousands of years. Band organization is often described as egalitarian: there is no formalized social stratification into upper and lower classes, no formalized or hereditary leadership, and no formalized monopolies of information and decision-making (Ibid: 269-270).

The people of Greater Sikkim (inclusive of the Limbuwan area, Chumbi, Har Chu and Ammo Chu valleys) were living in bands until the 6th century A.D; the Lepcha inhabiting of the present area of Sikkim, Chumbi Valley (at present under the Tibet Autonomous Region, China), Har Chu Valley and Ammo Chu Valley (present Bhutan) and Lapchan area of Nepal (present Ilam area of Nepal). In the 7th century A.D., Thekung Adek, consolidated the hunting-gathering Lepcha bands of these areas and declared himself as a Panu - a Tribal Religious and Administrative leader or king in 7th century.

Similarly, the Limboo people in the Limbuwan area of Nepal were in the band stage till the 6th century when the ten Limboo leaders fought with the other eight bands (leaders or kings), won the battle and consolidated their resources to form Limbuwan in the 7th century. They selected a leader from each of their clans and formed a social and administrative body known as "*Thibong Yakthum Tumyanghang*" (Ten Limboos Council) and ruled the country as a republic. Thus, they entered into the upper social stage of tribes from then onwards.

In both the above cases of bands, they lacked many institutions that we take for granted in modern societies. They had no permanent single base of residence. The whole group, instead of being partitioned among sub-groups or individuals, used the band's land jointly. There was no regular economic specialization, except by age and sex: for instance, all able-bodied individuals foraged for food. There were no formal institutions such as laws, police, and treaties, to resolve conflicts within and between bands. The Himalayan region being very rich in biodiversity of wild plants and animals, the people of this mountainous region remained hunter-gatherers for very long period.

In the absence of a population census, or linguistic and religious surveys during this period, no information on such aspects are available for Sikkim. However, it is certain that the western part of the Greater Sikkim area was inhabited mostly by the Limboos who were speakers of Limboo dialect and believers of Yumaism/ Yuma Samyo in faith. Ilam area of the West and most of the Eastern part of of the Greater Sikkim was inhabited by the Lepchas. They spoke Lepcha dialect and were believers of Boongthism and Munism (animist) by faith. (Chemjong, I.S. 1948; Diamond, J.1997: 258-292; Risley, H.H. 1894; Subba J.R. 1999; 2006; 2008; Vansittart, E. 1896).

2.2 People of Sikkim under Tribal social status (c. A.D. 700-1642)

Next to band of social stage is termed the "tribe", which differs in being larger and usually having fixed settlements. However, some tribes and even chiefdoms consist of herders who move seasonally. The tribal group shares language and culture. This political definition of "tribe" is often much smaller than what linguists and cultural anthropologists would define as a tribe. Evidence suggests that tribal organization began to emerge around 13,000 years ago for the first time in the Fertile Crescent and later in some other areas. The Greater Sikkim areas attained the social stage of "tribe" only by 7th century A.D. A prerequisite for living in settlements is either food production or a productive environment with essentially concentrated resources that can be hunted and gathered within a small area. That's why settlements, and by inference tribes, began to proliferate in the Fertile Crescent at that time, when climate changes and improved technology combined to permit abundant harvests of wild cereals as described in the previous chapter of food production.

A tribe differs from a band in settled residence and its larger numbers, consists of more than one formally recognized kinship group, termed clans, which exchange marriage partners. Land belongs to a particular clan, not to the whole tribe. However, the number of people in a tribe is still low enough that everyone knows everyone else by name and relationships. Diffusing potential problems of conflict resolution in tribes is that almost everyone is related to everyone else, by blood or marriage or both. These ties of relationships, binding all tribal members make police, laws, and since any two villages getting into an argument will share many kin, will apply pressure on them to keep it from turning violent.

Despite all of these differences between bands and tribes, many similarities remain. Tribes still have an informal, egalitarian system of government. Information and decision-making are communal. For instance, by the 7th century A.D. in the Greater Sikkim areas many villages or clans had someone known as the big-man or "*Thibong Yakthum Tumyanghang*" (tribal republic council) for social matters and "*Yahang*" (another tribal council) for religious matters in the case of the Limboos of Limbuwan area; or the most influential man of the village; or *Panu* for both social and religious matters in the case of Lepchas of present Sikkim and Lapchan areas; or a tribal leader or Incarnate Lamas in the case of Bhutia tribes in the present Sikkim and Chumbi areas by the 15th or early half of 16th century A.D. But that position is not a formal office to be filled and carries only limited powers. Such organizations or big-men had no independent decision-making authority, knew no diplomatic secrets, and could do no more than attempt to sway communal decisions. Such bodies or Big-men achieved that status by their own attributes; the position was not inherited.

Tribes also share with bands an egalitarian social system, without ranked lineages or classes. Not only is status not inherited; no member of a traditional tribe or band can become disproportionately wealthy by his or her own efforts, because each individual has debts and obligations to many others.

Like bands, tribes lack a bureaucracy, police force, and taxes. Their economy is based on reciprocal exchanges between individuals or families, rather than on a redistribution of tribute paid to some central authority. Economic specialization is slight: full-time crafts specialists are lacking, and every able-bodied adult participates in growing, gathering, or hunting food.

The Lepcha tribes, the Limboo tribes and the Bhutia tribes who came to the Greater Sikkim after the blood-brotherhood treaty of Kabi Lungchok in 1275 A.D. were at the social stage of "tribe" till 1642 A.D. The three ethnic tribal people of Sikkim continued this social stage from 7th century to 1642 A.D.

The better known Lepcha Panus (tribal kings) who led their community were Thekong Adek, the first Lepcha Ponu (7th-8th century), followed by Thup Athak (9th – 10th century), Thekong Tek (13th century), Rujo Panu (1353-1410 A.D.), Tarvey Panu (1425-1454 A.D.), Tarsong Panu (1454-1481 A.D.), Tar-eng Panu (1481-1520A.D.), Tarjyi Panu (1520-1564 A.D.),Tar-eak Panu (1564-1595 A.D.), and Thekong Mun Solong Panu (1595-1642 A.D.).

The popular Limboo Hangs (Kings/ tribal leaders) of Limbuwan region of the Greater Sikkim, who led their community in the 7th century were i) Thibong Yakthumba Tumyanghangs of the District (Yiok) namely: Samlupley Samba Hang of Tamber Yiok, Sesekkum Satrenu Hang of Poklabung Yiok, Akluk Hang of Pemajong Yiok, Thindolung Koya Hang of Hastapur Yiok, Sesiang Sereng Hang of Meringden Yiok, Niyaso Papo Hang of Pheden Yiok, Emibhu Khewa Hang of Takluk Yiok, Soyak Hang of Kurley Yiok, Ing

Hang of Chenlung Yiok, and Ime Hang of Angdang Yiok, ii) Bhuinphutta Hang (7th Century), iii) Mawrong Hang (7th century), iv) Mokani Hang (8th century), v) Uba Hang (849-865), vi) Mabo Hang (865-880), and vii) Sirijunga Hang (880-915).

Similarly, the popular Bhutia tribal leaders (Kings) who led their community after 1275 A. D. of Blood Brotherhood Treaty between the Lepcha Leader Thekong Tek and Khye-Bumsa in Sikkim were i) Khye Bumsa (13th century), ii) Mi-Ponrab (14th century), iii) Guru Tashi (15th century), iv) Jowo Nagpo (15th century), v) Jowo Aphag (16th century), and vi) Guru Tenzing (17th century). Phuntso Namgyal the first King of Sikkim was the son of Guru Tenzung, and with this listing, the Buddhist prophecy of 18 (eighteen) kings or Bhutia tribal leaders (inclusive of 12 kings/ Chiefdoms) of Namgyal Dynasty in Sikkim gets completed.

Population, linguistic and religious survey were not held during this period either; and thus no data is available for Sikkim on these aspects. However, it is certain that the area was inhabited by the Lepchas, the Limboos, the Magars and some Bhutias, atleast in the later part of this period. They were the speakers of their own dialects i.e. Lepcha, Limboo, Mangar, and Bhutia dialects; and followers of Boongthism- Munism (animist), Yumaism/ Yuma Samyo, Animists and Buddhist in faith respectively (Chemjong, I.S. 1948; Diamond, J.1997: 265-292; Risley, H.H. 1894; Subba J.R. 1994; 1999; 2006; 2008; Vansittart, E. 1896).

2.3 People of Sikkim under Chiefdom Social Status (c. A.D. 1642 - 1975)

Archaeological evidence reveals that chiefdoms arose by around 5,500 B.C. in the Fertile Crescent, by around 1,000 B.C. in Mesoamerica and the Andes. Sikkim entered into a Chiefdom social status in 1642 A.D. with the consecration of the first Chogyal Phuntsho Namgyal, at Narbugang, in present West Sikkim, and signing a tripartite treaty of "*Lho-Mon-Tsong-Sum*" by 8 (eight) Bhutia tribal leaders, 12 (twelve) Limboo tribal leaders and 4 (four) Lepcha tribal leaders in 1642 A.D. in Sikkim. As of 1492 A.D., chiefdoms were still widespread over much of the eastern United

States, in productive areas of South and Central America and Sub-Saharan Africa that had not yet been subsumed under native states, and in all of Polynesia. In the historic event of 1642 A.D. in Sikkim, the tribal leaders, Panu of the Lepchas, the Limboo leaders Hangs and the Bhutia leaders joined hands through the "*Lho-Mom-Tsong-Sum*" tripartite treaty, pooling their entire land resources and accepting Phuntso Namgyal (a Bhutia leader) as their first Chogyal (both temporal and spiritual king) of Sikkim and thus began the social stage of "Chiefdom" in Sikkim. Chiefdom thus started, continued upto 1975 in Sikkim. The twelve Chiefs or Chogyals of Sikkim who ruled the country for about 333 years, were: i) Phuntso Namgyal (1604-1670), ii) Tensung Namgyal (1644-1700), iii) Chagdor Namgyal (1700-1716), iv) Gyurmed Namgyal (1707-1733), v) Namgyal Phuntsog (1733-1780). vi) Tenzing Namgyal (1769-1793), vii) Tsugphud Namgyal (1785-1863), viii) Sridkyong Namgyal (1819-1874), ix) Thutop Namgyal (1860-1914), x) Sidkyong Tulku (1879-1914), xi) Tashi Namgyal (1893-1963), and xii) Palden Thondup Namgyal (1923-1982). But fully independent chiefdoms in other parts of the world had disappeared by the early twentieth century, because they tended to occupy prime land coveted by states.

As regards population size, chiefdoms were considerably larger than tribes, ranging from several thousand to several tens of thousands of people. That size created serious potential for internal conflict because a vast majority of people in the chiefdom were neither closely related by blood or marriage nor known by name. With the rise of chiefdoms around 7,500 years ago, people had to learn, for the first time in history, how to encounter strangers regularly without attempting to kill them.

Part of the solution to that problem was for one person, the Chief, Chogyal in the case of Sikkim, to exercise a monopoly on the right to use force. In contrast to a tribe's big-man or tribal council (*Tumyanghang/ Yahang*) or Panu as described above in the case of Sikkim, a chief held a recognized office, filled by hereditary right. Instead of the decentralized anarchy of a village meeting, the chief was a permanent centralized authority, and made all the significant decisions, and had a monopoly on critical information. Unlike big-man, Chiefs or the Chogyals in the case of Sikkim, could be recognized from afar by visible distinguishing features such as a royal dress or any such dress specified for the place or country. A commoner encountering a chief (Chogyal) was obliged to perform ritual marks of respect. The chief's (Chogyal's) orders might be transmitted through one or two levels of bureaucrats (Kazis or Officials), many of whom were themselves low-ranked chiefs. However, in contrast to state bureaucrats, chiefdom bureaucrats had generalized rather than specialized roles.

For instance, in Sikkim, the chiefs (Chogyals) were from the Bhutia tribe. The Bhutias have descended from the chief families of four known as *Tong-du-ruzhis* plus chiefdom families of eight known as *Beb-tsan-Gyat*. All the council of ministers (*Kashag*) and Prime Ministers (*Changzot*) of the Chogyals were constituted from these 12 Bhutia families, and the entire political, administrative and social matters were in the hands of these councillors. The country was divided into 12 *dzongs* (districts). The Chogyal selected 12 Lepchas from among the superior families of Lepchas of Sikkim to serve as *Jongpens* (District Administrative Officers). They connived with the chief hereditary Bhutia families (12 Families described above) and exploited the commoners and were a separate class of people known as the *Kazis*, who were responsible for revenue collection and maintaining law and order in their respective jurisdictions. Throughout the period of the Namgyal Dynasty (about 333 years), the common people, mainly from the Nepali ethnic group and common Lepchas, were exploited in various ways by the *Kashag*, Kazis, landlords, Thekadars, Mandals and Karbaries. The economic condition of the common people was very miserable.

In 1740 A.D., the Sikkim administration (then under Rabden Sherpa Gyalpo) imposed a fixed tax-system of revenue such as *Bah-pa, Zolung, Tshong-skyed* etc. on the farmers. In 1898 the Chogyal introduced Zamindari and Thikadari system and taxed the farmers heavily. A preference rate of 8 *anna* (half a rupee) per *pathi* of seed sown was charged to the Bhutia and Lepcha farmers, while the Nepali ethnic group inclusive of Limboo farmers were charged 14 *anna* (87.5% of rupee). All the Lepcha and Bhutia farmers were allowed to graze three cows free of charge while the Nepali ethnic group inclusive of Limboo farmers were taxed 8 *annas* (half a rupee) per cattle head. The Nepali farmers were also taxed Rs.6.75 per annum as rent for their dwellings (*Dhurikhazana*). In addition to the above, farmers from the Nepali ethnic group had to contribute free labour in the form of *Kalobhari, Jharlangi, Kuruwa* etc. compulsory to the Government, Kazis, Landlords, Mandals, and Karbaries. In addition to the above they had to then pay *Theki-Bethi.* Throughout the chiefdom period of about 333 years, the Namgyal Dynasty's rule was diarchic and extremely exploitative to the common people especially the Limboos, common Lepchas, and Nepali ethnic group farmers ((Bhadra, M. 1992: 74-80; Subba, J.R. 1999; 2008: 58-66).

Due to this exploitative nature of the Chogyal regime, the Limboo tribes of Limbuwan beyond the Singhalila range withdrew their allegiance and declared independence, reverting back to becoming a "tribe". This was at the time of the fourth Chogyal, Gyurmed Namgyal (1707-1733), and Limbuan remained independent till the Gorkha invasions of 1774 A.D. (Subba, J.R.1999; 2008: 51-52; Vansittart, E. 1896).

The people were not happy with the Chogyal's government. With the internal urge of the common people to break free from this exploitation regime pulling at one end and the play of external forces at the other extreme, major portions of Greater Sikkim (as established in 1642 A.D.) disintegrated, territories were lost to annexation in eight phases during the chiefdom of Chogyals (c. A.D. 1642 to 1975): i) *Mon-Long-Kha-bzi* area by Bhutan in 1700 A.D., ii) Limbuwan area in 1730s, iii) Eastern Hills and Terai areas by the Gorkha in 1774, iv) Occupation of West District of Sikkim by Gorkhas for 25 years (1889 to 1814), v) Annexation of Darjeeling area by the British in 1835, vi) Annexation of the Terai Region and Hill areas of Sikkim by British in 1860, vii) Annexation of Chumbi Valley by China in 1890, and viii) Merger of the remaining area of Sikkim into the Indian union in 1975 (Subba, J.R. 1999; 2008: 50-58).

A Chiefdom's large population in a small area requires plenty of food, obtained by agriculture in most cases, or by hunting-gathering in a few especially rich areas. For example, the people of Sikkim were primarily hunter-gatherers upto 1880s. It is only in the last decade of 1890s that the British administration (J.C.White, Assistant Political Officer) started settling its own people in addition to the Nepalese from Nepal by clearing the forests for food production, labour required by them for trade and state fund raising by taxation. Sikkim had never been a surplus food producer but supplemented its requirements through mixed farming and hunting gathering of rich biodiversity of wild plants and animals. However, it was not possible to depend 100% on outside sources. Minimum production of food was essential to feed the general people of Sikkim. The British policy of settlement of the people from Nepal was opposed by many elite close to the then Chogyal, Thutob Namgyal (1860-1914). But a few kleptocrats, along with White promoted the settlement. This policy introduced many tribes of Nepali ethnic groups such as Gurung, Khombu-Rai, Yakkha, Tamang, Khasa (Bahun, Chettri, Kami, Damai, Sarki), Majhi, Newar, Thami, Bhujel, Jogi/ Sanyasi, Sherpa, Magar, Thakuri and also more Limboo people from Nepal in Sikkim. Although, the boundaries of Nepal, Sikkim, Bhutan and India were never watertight, and whoever wanted could freely move and settle in Sikkim with the mutual consent of the residents since ancient times, with the settlement policy of the government from 1890s, the migration of Nepali population became legalized and extensive. Also, during the 25-year Gorkha occupation of West Sikkim (1789-1814), more and more people of Nepali ethnic groups mentioned above migrated to West Sikkim and remained there with the land when it was returned by Nepal to British India and thence to Sikkim as per the Treaty of Sugouli in 1815, and then again through the Titalyia Treaty in 1817. Along with the people came their belief systems, religions, cultures etc. Thus, by the first quarter of the nineteenth century, the Nepali ethnic community which had migrated to Sikkim formed the majority of the population in Sikkim.

Further, luxury goods, comprising of better food, vegetables and fruits, clothing, implements, specialized crafts products and rare objects obtained by long-distance trade were reserved for chiefs and their hereditary families and the British Official residing in Sikkim. For their continuous supply, the elite kleptocrats of the chiefdom and the British administration encouraged the settlement of plainsmen business communities in Sikkim, especially Marwaris, Bengalis, Biharis etc. right from 1890s onwards. Even these groups arrived with their religions, cultures and customs. By the first quarter of twentieth century these business communities made up a considerable size of population.

A modern education system was introduced from the 1920s onwards. Major reforms in the educational system, undertaken through the 1940s to 60s, required the services of qualified teachers who came from South Indian states like Kerala, Tamil Nadu, etc. This policy resulted in the arrival of many South Indian families to Sikkim. Thus, by the 1960s, the people of Sikkim, as with any modern society, constituted a mixture of many races such as Aryan, Dravidian, Mongolian, the aboriginal Lepchas, Limboos, migrant Bhutias and Nepalese .

Like tribes, chiefdoms consisted of multiple hereditary lineages living at one site. However, the chief's lineage in the case of Sikkim as mentioned above, had hereditary perquisites. In effect, the society was divided into hereditary chiefs, favoured tribes and commoner classes, divided in Sikkim into Bhutia, Lepcha and Nepali ethnic groups, and subdivided further into many hierarchically ranked lineages such as *Tong-du-ruzhis, Beb-tsan-Gyat, Changzots, Koshags, Kazis, Zamindars, Thekadars, Mandals, Karbaries* etc., each concentrating its marriages within its own lineage.

The eleventh Chogyal Sir Tashi Namgyal introduced a diarchic policy of electoral process in 1953 by reserving seats on parity basis between Bhutia-Lepcha and Nepali ethnic groups for the constitution of the State Council for the first time. He de-recognized the special identity of the Limboos as distinguished during the establishment of the Himalayan kingdom in 1642 A.D. and clubbed the Limboos with the later Nepali migrants. The provision was based on the "Parity Formula" whereby State Council Seats were reserved equally between the Nepali ethnic group comprising 75% of the population and the Bhutia-Lepcha population that made up the rest [25%]. In 1967, however, one seat was reserved for the Limboos, reflecting a special status on the Limboos of Sikkim. The Limboo seat was however abolished with the 8 May 1973 agreement, which clubbed the Limboos with the Nepali ethnic group forever (Bhadra, M, 1992:85; Subba, J.R. 1999; 2008:67-68).

Thus, the chiefdoms introduced the dilemma fundamental to all centrally governed, non-egalitarian societies. At best, they do good by providing expensive services impossible to contract on individual basis. At worst, they function unabashedly as kleptocracies, transferring net wealth from the commoners to the upper classes. These noble and selfish functions are inextricably linked, although some governments emphasize more of one function over the other. The difference between a kleptocrat and a wise statesman, between a robber baron and a public benefactor, is merely one degree: a matter of just how large a percentage of the tribute extracted from producers is retained by the elite, and how much of the tribute is redistributed for public benfit. For example, we can compare a Kleptocrat Kazi (*Jongpen*/ district administrator) of Chogyal's time having more than a thousand hectares land per family even now and the personal possessions of a District Collector of any of the districts of today's Sikkim.

Whether a chiefdom or a state, Kleptocrats throughout the ages have restored to a mixture of four solutions:

(i) Disarm the populace, and arm the elite;

(ii) Make the masses happy by redistributing much of the tribute or fund received from the source in popular ways as in the case of Sikkim today;

(iii) Use the monopoly of force to promote happiness, by maintaining public order and curbing violence; and

(iv) The remaining way for Kleptocrats to gain public support is to construct an ideology or religion justifying kleptocracy. Bands and tribes already had supernatural beliefs, just as modern established religions do. But the supernatural beliefs of bands and tribes did not serve to justify central authority, justify transfer of wealth, or maintain peace between unrelated individuals. When supernatural beliefs gained those functions and become institutionalized, they were thereby transformed into what we term a religion. The chief may either combine the offices of political leader and priest in a single person, as in the case of the Chogyals of Sikkim, or support a separate group of kleptocrats (that is, priests) whose function is to provide ideological justification for the chiefs as in the case of India today. It is astonishing that the Constitution of India in a special Article inserted for Sikkim [371 F], continues to support this type of kleptocracy. That is why chiefdoms or State Heads devote so much collected tribute to constructing temples, Gumpas, Mangkhims and other public works, which serve as centres of the official religion and visible signs of the chief's power.

Population census for the present area of Sikkim was started in 1891. Since then, the population data is available on a decadal basis.

Temporal changes in population 1891-1971 are as follows:

Year	*Male*	*Female*	*Total*	*Sex ratio (f/1000 m)*	*Decadal % variations*	*Density sq. km*
1891	11,589	10,563	30,458	912		4
1901	39,795	28,219	59,014	709	93.75	8
1911	45,059	42,861	87,920	951	48.98	12
1921	41,492	40,229	81,721	970	(-) 7.05	12
1931	55,825	53,983	109,808	967	34.75	15
1941	63,289	58,231	121,520	920	10.66	17
1951	72,210	65,515	137,725	907	13.34	19
1961	85,193	76,996	162,189	904	17.76	23
1971	112,662	97,181	209,843	863	29.38	30

Sources: Census of India.

Although tribe-wise/ caste-wise data, linguistic and religious data are not available as of this period. A number of tribes and castes were added up in the present areas of Sikkim, specially Bhutias from the Tibet region of China after 1642 A.D., Nepalese including more of Limboos from Nepal after occupation of West Sikkim by Gorkhas for 25 years after 1789 (1789-1814 A.D.), and especially after 1890s due to Nepali-settlement policy of the British Administration. The business community and service industry professionals, specially Marwaris, Biharis, Bengalis, Malayalis, etc. from the plains of India arrived to cater to the business of essential commodities, school teachers, and labour force required for development especially after the 1890s encouraged by the British Administration, and again after 1950s when Plan Development started in Sikkim.

Hence, the population of Sikkim by the later period of Chiefdomship compised of the Hill communities namely: Lepchas, Bhutias, Sherpas, Limboos, Khombu-Rais, Yakhas, Sunuwars, Magars, Gurungs, Tamangs, Bhujels, Thamis, Khasas (Bahun, Chettri, Kami, Damai, Sarki), Thakuris, Jogis/Sanyasis, Majhis, and Newars; Indian plain communities such as Marwaries, Biharies, Bengalies, Punjabis, Kerelites, etc. All these tribes spoke their own languages or dialects but Nepali was the *lingua franca* of Sikkim. English and Tibetan languages were adopted for official purposes. The important religions adopted were Hinduism, Buddhism, Christianity, Islam, Boongthism-Munism, Yuma Samyo and animism. Thus, by the end of Chiefdomship in 1975, the population of Sikkim comprised of a multilingual, milticultural, multiethnic and a secular communities broadly divided into Lepcha, Bhutia, Nepali and plains-men ethnic groups (Risley, H.H. 1894; Subba, J.R. 1994; 1999; 2006; 2008).

2.4 People of Sikkim under Modern Society (1975 A.D.)

The most familiar political, economic, and social institutions to us nowadays are the states, which now rule all of the world's land area except for Antarctica. Many early states and all modern ones have had literate elite though an increasing number of modern states now have literate masses as well. Vanished states tended to leave visible archaeological hallmarks such as ruins of temples with standardized designs, at least four levels of settlement sizes, and pottery styles covering tens of thousands of square miles. Archeological evidence reveals that states arose around 3,700 B.C. in Mesopotamia and around 300 B.C. in Mesoamerica, over 2,000 years ago in the Andes, China, and Southeast Asia including India, and over 1,000 years ago in West Africa. In modern times, the formation of states out of chiefdoms has been observed repeatedly. Thus, more information about past states and their formation is known today than is know about past chiefdoms, tribes and bands.

So far, in as much as Sikkim is concerned, the State stepped into Associate Statehood status of India in 1974 and finally as a full-fledged statehood status only in 1975 when it merged into the Indian Union as the 22nd State of India. However, constitutionally Sikkim still retains some traces of its chiefdom status such as retention and reservation of a seat in the legislative assembly for religious priest (*Sangha*), disproportionate reservation of Bhutia-Lepcha seats (41%), and no provision for reservation of Scheduled Tribe seats in the State Legislative Assembly as yet in Sikkim.

Proto-states extended many features of large paramount chiefdoms. They continue the increase in size from bands to tribes to chiefdoms. While a Chiefdom's populations ranges to a few ten thousands, the populations of most modern states exceed one million, and China's exceeds one billion. Early states had a hereditary leader with a title equivalent to king, like a super paramount chief and exercising an even greater monopoly of information, decision-making, and power. Central control is more far-reaching, and economic redistribution in the form of tribute (taxes) more extensive in states than in chiefdoms. Economic specialization is more extreme, to the point where today, not even farmers remain self-sufficient. Hence the effect on society is catastrophic when state government's collapse.

Many, perhaps most, early states adopted slavery on a much larger scale than did chiefdoms. State governments have several separate departments, each with its own hierarchy, to handle water management, taxes, military draft, and so on. Laws, a judiciary, and police have increasingly formalized internal conflict resolution within states. The laws are often written because many states have had literate elites. Early state had a state religion and standardized temples. Many early kings were considered divine and were accorded special treatment in innumerable respects.

All these features of states carry to an extreme the developments that led from tribes to chiefdoms. In addition, though, states have diverged from chiefdoms in several new directions. The most fundamental such distinction is that states are organized on political and territorial lines, not on the kinship lines that defined bands, tribes, and simple chiefdoms. Furthermore, bands and tribes always, and usually also chiefdoms, consist of a single ethnic and linguistic group. States, especially the so-called empires formed by amalgamation or conquest of states, are invariably multiethnic and multilingual. State bureaucrats are not selected solely on the basis of kinship, as in chiefdoms, but are professionals selected at least partly on the basis of training and ability. In later states, the leadership often become nonhereditary.

For instance, Sikkim is now multilingual, multiethnic, multicultural, and secular democratic 22nd State of India. Although, some remnants of chiefdom still remain since it is still a young state, the Constitution of India and the laws protect every individual's fundamental rights. It is out of context to elaborate the details of this line of argument in this book but details of Sikkim's history, culture and customs can be gleaned from my book entitled "History, Culture and Customs of Sikkim" published in 2008.

3. The Evolution of the Modern Societies

In the early human societies, the smaller, less complex units were replaced by larger, more complex ones. Obviously, this is no more than an average long-term trend, with innumerable shifts in either direction: 1,000 amalgamations for 999 reversals. For instance, the history of Greater Sikkim's existence in 1642 A.D. and then its disintegration in various phases, the former USSR, Yugoslavia, and Czechoslovakia, Alexander of Macedon's empire over 2,000 years ago. More complex units do not always conquer less complex ones but many succumb to them, as in the case of Sikkim merging into the Indian Union, or how the Roman and Chinese empires were overrun by "barbarians" and Mongol chiefdoms, respectively. But the long-term trend has been toward large, complex societies, culminating into states.

One reason for the states' triumphs over simpler entities when the two collide is that states usually enjoy an advantage in weaponry and other technology and a large numerical advantage in population. But there are also two other potential advantages inherent in chiefdoms and states. First, a centralized decision maker has the advantage of concentrating troops and resources. Second, the official religions and patriotic fervor of many states make their troops willing to fight to the end. The latter willingness is one strongly programmed into us citizens of modern states by our schools and religious priests and governments that we overlook the radical break it marks from previous human history. Every state or a country has its slogan urging its citizens to be prepared to die if necessary for the state and its cause: Britain's "For King and Country," Spain's "Por Diosy Espana," and so on. Similar sentiments motivated 16th century Aztec warriors: "There is nothing like death in war, nothing like the flowery death so precious to Him (the Aztec national god Huitzilopochtli) who gives life: far off I see it, my heart yearns for it!"

Such sentiments are unthinkable in bands and tribes and this attitude severely limits the military options of tribes compared with state societies. Naturally, what makes patriotic and religious fanatics such dangerous opponents is not the death of the fanatics themselves, but their willingness to accept the deaths of a fraction of their number in order to annihilate or crush their infidel enemy. Fanaticism in war, of the type that drove recorded Christian and Islamic conquests, was probably unknown to Earth until chiefdoms and states emerged over the last 6,000 years (Diamond, J. 1997: 265-292).

3.1 Theories of State Origins

In many moments in history, states have arisen independently or, as cultural anthropologists say "pristinely," that is, in the absence of any preexisting surrounding states. Pristine state origins took place at least once, possibly many times, on each of the continents except Australia and North America. Prehistoric states included those of Mesopotamia, North China, the Nile and Indus Valleys, Mesoamerica, the Andes, and West Africa. Native states in contrast with European states have arisen repeatedly from chiefdoms in the past three centuries in Madagascar, Hawaii, Tahiti, Sikkim, and many parts of Africa. Chiefdoms have arisen pristinely even more often, in all of the same regions and in North America's Southeast and Pacific Northwest, the Amazon, Polynesia, Sikkim in 1642, and Sub-Saharan Africa. All these origins of complex societies give us a rich database to understand their development. Diamond, J. (1997) has pointed out the various theories put forward on the origins of Modern States are as follows:

3.11 The Social Contact Theory

Aristotle considered states the natural condition of human society, requiring no explanation. His error was understandable, because all the societies with which he would have been acquainted, Greek societies of the fourth century B.C., were states. However, in 1492 A.D. much of the world was instead organized into chiefdoms, tribes, or bands. State formation does demand an explanation.

3.12 Jean Jacques Rousseau Theory

The French philosopher Jean Jacques Rousseau speculated that states are formed by a social contract, a rational decision reached when people calculated their self-interest, came to the agreement that they would be better off in a state than in simpler societies, and voluntarily did away with their simpler societies. This is the most familiar theory. But observation and historical records have failed to uncover a single case of a state's being formed in that ethereal atmosphere of dispassionate farsightedness. Smaller units do not voluntarily abandon their sovereignty and merge into larger units. They do so only by conquest, or under external duress, as seen in Sikkim in 1975.

3.13 Irrigation or Hydraulic Management Theory

This theory is still popular with some historians and economists and sets out from the undoubted fact that in Mesopotamia, North China and Mexico, large-scale irrigation systems began to be constructed around the time that states started to emerge. The theory also notes that any big, complex system for irrigation or hydraulic management requires a centralized bureaucracy to construct and maintain it. However, this theory is subject to the same objections leveled against social contract theories in general.

3.14 Theory of Population Density or Population Pressure

The size of the regional population is the strongest single predictor of social complexity. Bands number a few dozen individuals, tribes a few hundred, chiefdoms a few thousand to a few tens of thousands, and states generally over about 50,000. In addition to that coarse correlation between regional population size and type of society (band, tribe, and so on), there is a finer trend, within each of those categories, between population and societal complexity: for instance, that chiefdoms with large populations prove to be the most centralized, stratified, and complex ones. These correlations suggest strongly that regional population size or population density or population pressure has something to do with the formation of complex societies. But the correlations do not tell us precisely how population variables function in a chain of cause and effect whose outcome is a complex society.

3.2 Change of simpler societies to complex societies as the regional population increases

Large or dense populations arise faster only under conditions of food production, or at least under exceptionally productive conditions for hunting-gathering. Some productive hunter-gatherer societies reached the organizational level of chiefdoms, but none reached the level of states: all states nourish their citizens by food production. Intensified food production and social complexity stimulate each other by autoanalysis. That is, population growth leads to social complexity by mechanism, while social complexity in turn leads to intensified food production and thereby to population growth. Complex centralized societies are uniquely capable of organizing public works, long-distance trade, and activities of different groups of economic specialists. Diamond (1997) pointed out that all of these capabilities of centralized societies have fostered intensified food production and hence population growth throughout history. Conversely, Sikkim never had intensified food production but its social complexity was brought about by an influx of the people from outside and other external forces.

Intensified food production and social complexity stimulate each other by autocatalysis. That is, population growth leads to social complexity, by mechanisms while societal complexity in turn leads to intensified food production and thereby to population growth. Complex centralized societies are uniquely capable of organizing public works, long-distance trade, and activities of different groups of economic specialists. All of these capabilities of centralized societies have fostered intensified food production and hence population growth throughout history. In addition, food production contributes in at least three ways to specific features of complex societies.

(i) **First,** it involves seasonally pulsed inputs of labour. When the harvest has been stored, the farmers' labour becomes available for a centralized political authority to harness – in order to build public works.

(ii) **Second,** food production may be organized so as to generate stored food surpluses, which permit economic specialization and social stratification. The surplus can be used to feed all tiers of a complex society: the chiefs, bureaucrats, and other members of the elite; the scribes, craftsmen, and other non-food-producing specialists; and the farmers themselves, during times that they are drafted to construct public works.

(iii) **Finally,** food production permits or requires people to adopt sedentary lifestyles, which is a prerequisite for accumulating substantial possessions, developing elaborate technology and crafts, and constructing public works. Thus, food production, which increases population size, also acts in many ways to make features of complex societies possible.

The band or tribal organization just does not work for societies of hundreds of thousands of people. One reason is the problem of conflict between unrelated strangers. That problem grows astronomically as the number of people making up the society increases. Relationships within a band of 20 people involve only 190 two-person interactions (20 people times 19 divided by 2), but a band of 2,000 would have 1,999,000 dyads. Each of these dyads represents a potential timebomb that could explode in a murderous argument. Each murder in a band or a tribal society usually leads to an attempted revenge killing, starting one more unending cycle of murder and counter-murder that destabilizes the society.

In a band, where everyone is closely related to everyone else, people related simultaneously to both quarreling parties step in to mediate quarrels. In a tribe, where many people are still close relatives and everyone at least knows everybody else by name, mutual relatives and mutual friends mediate the quarrel. But once the threshold of "several hundred" has been crossed, increasing numbers of dyads become pairs of unrelated strangers. When strangers fight, few people present will be friends or relatives of both combatants, with a self-interest is stopping the fight. Instead, many onlookers will be friends or relatives of only one combatant and will side with that person escalating the two-person fight into a general brawl. Hence a large society that continues to leave conflict resolution to all of its members is guaranteed to blow up. This factor alone could explain why societies of thousands can exist only if they develop centralized authority to monopolize force and resolve conflicts.

A second reason is the growing impossibility of communal decision making with increasing population size. Decision-making by the entire adult population is possible in small societies. News and information quickly spread to everyone; everyone can hear everyone else in a meeting and everyone who wants to speak has the opportunity to do so. But all these prerequisites for communal decision-making become unattainable in much larger communities. A group meeting is no way to resolve issues for a group of thousands of people. Hence, a large society must be structured and centralized if it is to reach decisions effectively.

A third reason involves economic considerations. Any society requires means to transfer goods between its members. In small societies with few pairs of members, the resulting necessary transfers of goods can be arranged directly between pairs of individuals or families through reciprocal exchange. But the same mathematics that makes direct pair-wise conflict resolution inefficient in large societies, also makes direct pair-wise economic transfers inefficient. Large societies can function economically only if they have a redistributive economy in addition to a reciprocal economy. Goods in excess of an individual's needs must be transferred from the individual to a centralized authority, which then redistributes the goods to individuals with deficits.

A final consideration mandating complex organization for large societies has to do with population densities. As population density increases, the territory of that band-sized population of a few dozen would shrink to a small area, with more and more of life's necessities having to be obtained from outside the area. Thus, considerations of conflict resolution, decision making, economics, and space converge in requiring large societies to be centralized (Diamond, J. 1997: 265-292).

3.3 Evolution Processes of Large and Complex Societies

As pointed out by Diamond (1997), evolution of small, simple societies into large, complex, centralized conflict resolution, decision-making, economic redistribution, and kleptocratic religion partly depends upon evolutionary reasoning. The societies classified in the same category are not all identical to each other because humans and human groups are infinitely diverse. For example, among bands and tribes, the big-men of some are inevitably more charismatic, powerful, and skilled in reaching decisions than the big-men of others. Among large tribes, those with stronger big-men and hence greater centralization tend to have an advantage over those with lesser centralization. Tribes that resolve conflicts poorly tend to disintegrate again into bands, while ill-governed chiefdoms blow apart into smaller chiefdoms or tribes. Societies with effective conflict resolution, sound decision-making, and harmonious economic redistribution can develop better technology, concentrate their military power, seize larger and more productive territories and crush autonomous smaller societies one by one.

Thus, competition between societies at one level of complexity tends to lead to societies to occupy the next level of complexity if conditions permit. Tribes conquer or combine with tribes to reach the size of chiefdoms, which conquer or combine with other chiefdoms to reach the size of states, which conquer or combine with other states to become empires. More generally, large units potentially enjoy an advantage over individual small units if the large units can solve the problems that come with their larger sizes, such as perennial threats, and attendant problems associated with economic integration.

The amalgamation of smaller units into larger ones has often been documented historically or archaeologically. Contrary to Rousseau, such amalgamations never occur by a process of unthreatened little societies freely deciding to merge with the aim to promote the happiness of their citizens. Leaders of little societies, as of big ones, are jealous of their independence and prerogatives. Amalgamation occurs instead in either of two ways: by merger under the threat of external force, or by actual conquest.

Merger under the threat of external forces is well illustrated by the formation of the Cherokee Indian confederation in the U.S. Southeast. The Cherokees were originally divided into 30 or 40 independent chiefdoms, each consisting of a village of about 400 people. Increasing White settlements led to conflicts between Cherokees and Whites. In response, the Cherokee chiefdoms gradually found themselves compelled to join into a single confederacy in the course of the 18th century. The Cherokee confederacy was thus formed not by conquest but by the amalgamation of previously jealous smaller entities, which merged only when threatened with destruction by powerful external forces. In much the same way, in an example of state formation, the White American colonies themselves, one of which - Georgia - had precipitated the formation of the Cherokee state.

The other mode of formation of complex societies, besides merger under threat of external force, is merger by conquest. A well-documented example is the origin of the Zulu state in southern

Africa. When first observed by White settlers, the Zulus were divided into dozens of little chiefdoms. In the 1700s, as population pressure rose, fighting between the chiefdoms became increasingly intense. Among all those chiefdoms, Dingiswayo developed a superior centralized military organization and conquered other chiefdoms, and consequently formed a Zulu state by expanding judicial system, policing, and ceremonies. This Zulu example of a state formed by conquest can be multiplied almost indefinitely. Native states whose formation from chiefdoms happened to be witnessed by Europeans in the 18th and 19th centuries include Polynesian Hawaiin state, the Polynesian Tahitian state, the Merina state of Madagascar, Lesotho and Swazi and other southern African states, Roman state, Macedonian Empire etc.

All these examples illustrate that wars, or threats of war, have played a key role in most, if not all, amalgamation of societies. But wars, even between mere bands, have been a constant fact of human history. However, formation of complex societies is somehow linked to population pressure and population pressure started building up only after food production started around 13,000 years ago. War tends to cause amalgamations of societies when populations are dense and not when they are sparse. The fate of defeated peoples depends on population density with three possible outcomes:

(i) Where population densities are very low, as is usual in regions occupied by hunter-gatherer bands, survivors of a defeated group need only move farther away from their enemies. For instance, the Lepchas of Chumbi valley ran away to the main region of Sikkim when Khye-Bumsa waged war and captured the valley in the 13th century. The mainland Lepcha people of Sikkim however had nowhere to go and hence they established a blood-brotherhood treaty (friendship treaty) with the intruder – Khye-Bumsa in 1275 A.D. and remained exploited by the victors amalgamating their society into the victorious tribes.

(ii) Where population densities are moderate, as in regions occupied by food-producing tribes, no large vacant areas remain to which survivors of a defeated band can flee. But tribal societies without intensive food production have no employment for slaves and do not produce large enough food surpluses to be able to yield much tribute. Hence, the victors have no use for survivors of a defeated tribe, unless to take the women in marriage. The defeated men are killed, and their territory occupied by the victors.

(iii) Where population densities are high, as in regions occupied by states or chiefdoms, the defeated still have nowhere to flee, but the victors now have two options for exploiting them while leaving them alive. Because chiefs and state societies have economic specialization, the defeated can be used as slaves, as commonly happened in biblical times. Alternatively, because many such societies have intensive food production systems capable of yielding large surpluses, the victors can leave the defeated in place but deprive them of political autonomy, make them pay regular tribute in food or goods, and amalgamate their society into the victorious state or chiefdom. This has been the usual outcome of battles associated with founding of states or empires throughout recorded history.

Thus, food production, competition and diffusion between societies as the ultimate causes, via chains of causation that differed in detail but invariably involved large dense populations and sedentary lifestyles, led us into crafting centralized organization leading to a modern society (Diamond, J. 1997: 265-292).

3.4 Composition of Modern Society in mountainous Sikkim

The modern society in this mountainous Sikkim today comprised of the followings:

(a) Hill Tribes:

The hill tribes comprised of Lepchas, Bhutias, Sherpas, the Ancient Kiratas (Limboos, Khombu-Rais, Yakhas), the Communities Analogous to Kiratas (Sunuwars, Magars, Gurungs, Tamangs, Bhujels, Thamis), the Khasas (Bhahuns, Chettries, Kamis, Damais, Sarkis), the communities analogous to Khasas (Thakuris, Jogi/ Sanyasis, Majhis), and Newars.

(b) Plains-men

The plains-men comprises of Marwaries, Biharies, Bengalies, Punjabies, Kerelites, Madrasies, etc. More and more plains-men were added up after Sikkim was integrated into the Indian union in 1975 A.D onwords due to increase in developmental activities.

Temporal changes in population 1891 - 1971 are as follows:

Year	*Male*	*Female*	*Total*	*Sex ratio (f/1000 m)*	*Decadal % variations*	*Density sq. km*
1971	112,662	97,181	209,843	863	29.38	30
1981	172,440	143,945	316,385	835	50.77	45
1991	216,427	190,030	406,457	878	28.47	57
2001	288,217	252,276	540,851	875	33.06	76

Source: Census of India 1971-2001

Between 1971-1981, there was a substantial increase in population especially in the urban areas. This can be attributed to the merger of Sikkim with the Indian Union and the subsequent in-migration triggered by largescale development activities in the State. In the following decade (1981-1991), population grew at a much lower rate of 2.85% per annum, whereas in 1991-2001, the rate of growth was higher again at 3.30% per annum. This is again due to in-migration from neighbouring state and Nepal due to accelerated development activities in the State after Mr P.K. Chamling assumed the Chief Ministership in Sikkim.

According to the census of 1981, the speakers of different languages were as follows:

Language	*No. of speakers*	*Remarks*
Nepali (Khas-Kura)	1,92,891	Schedule VIII
Lepcha	22,391 other than	specified in sch. VIII
Bhutia	21,548	"
Limboo	17,922	"
Sherpa	10,726	"
Tibetan	4,149	"
Other languages	18,899	"

Other Schedule VIII languages languages	19,570	Other	Indian

Source: Census of India 1981; Subba, J.R.& Subba , B.M.(1994).

Out of the total population of 316,262 in the State, 212,461 are the speakers of Schedule VIII languages after inclusion of Nepali, constituting 68,92%. The rest constituting 31.08% to total are speakers of other languages.

Similarly, Religious composition of Sikkim in 1981 census was as follows:

Name of Religion	*Population*	*% of total Population*
Hindus	212,780	67.25
Buddhists	90,848	28.71
Christians	7,015	2.22
Muslims	3,241	1.03
Sikhs	322	0.10
Jain	108	0.03
Other religions	1,987	0.63
Religion not stated	64	0.03

Census of India 1981;J.R.& Subba B.M.(1994):16-20

Hindus form a majority of Sikkim with 67.25 per cent, followed by Buddhists at 28.71 per cent, Christians 2.22 per cent, Muslims 1.03 per cent and other religions in negligible percentages.

Based on the 2004 voters' list of Sikkim, the projected ethnic-wise population of Sikkim during 2004 was as follows:

Name of Tribes/castes	*Projected Population*	*% of total*
Lepcha	48,811	8.46
Bhutia	74,164	12.39
Sherpa	25,808	4.31
Limboo	54,750	9.15
Khombu-Rai/Yakha	75,708	13.54
Sunuwar	2,091	-
Magar	13,373	2.25
Gurung	39,042	6.52
Tamang	35,194	5.88

Thami	650	-
Khasas	1,26,984	26.87
Higher Khasas a. Bahun	50,395	8.42
b. Chettri	75,722	12.65
Lower Khasas		
(Kami, Damai, Sarki, Majhi)	36,868	5.80
Newar	26,082	4.26
Muslim	2,649	
Other (Plains-men)	29,300	4.89

Source: Subba, J.R. 2008; Voterlist 2004 (x 2.14)

Thus, the modern society of Sikkim comprises of multi-lingual, multi-cultural and secular democrats representing diversity of ethnicity.

3.5 The Evolutionary process of Modern society in the mountainous Sikkim:

The evolutionary process of the Modern Society in the mountainous Sikkim can be divided into three distinct phases as follows:

(a) Evolution of Human ancestors

4.0 million years ago:	Our ancestors started upright walking in Africa for the first time;
2.5 million years ago:	Our ancestors started using stone tools in Africa for the first time;

(ii) Evolution of Modern Thinking Man

50,000 years ago :	Evolution of Modern Thinking Man took place in Africa;
10,000 years ago:	Modern man started food production by domestication of wild plants and animals;
4,000 years ago:	Modern man invented Alphabet (2000 B.C.) and thereby writing system for the first time;

(iii) Evolution of modern Society in the mountainous Sikkim

? - 700 A.D.:	Period of Band life. Modern man of mountainous Sikkim was living in a Band Social life;

c. A.D. 700 - 1642	Period of Tribal Social Status; Modern man of mountainous Sikkim abandoned nomadic band life and entered into a Tribal-lifealong with hunting -gathering.
c. A.D. 600 - 700	Modern man of mountainous Sikkim started shifting cultivation with local domesticates and crops domesticated elsewhere as an alternative means of livelihood.
c. A.D.700 -900	Modern man of mountainous Sikkim started developing scripts for their own languages.
c. A.D. 1642	Modern man of mountainous Sikkim started a Chiefdom life
c. A.D. 1890s ...	Modern man of mountainous Sikkim started settled agriculture.
c. A.D. 1975	Emengence of Modern Society. Modern man of mountainous Sikkim started a State-life or living in a modern civilised society.

5

SARD-M in Mountainous Moder Sikkim

It was in the 2nd week of October 2005 that I was informed by the International Centre for Integrated Mountain Development (ICIMOD), Kathmandu, Nepal, that FAO has offered a Consultancy work for the FAO (Food and Agriculture Organization, Rome, Italy) sponsored SARD-M (Sustainable Agriculture and Rural Development in Mountainous region) project to be conducted in India (Sikkim), and have to attend the workshop meeting on 17th -18th October 2005 at Kathmandu. It was a great opportunity to learn about SARD-M and we were briefed thoroughly by SARD-M expert of FAO Dr.Takashi Takahatake, mountain experts Dr. N.S. Jodha, Dr. E. Sharma, Dr. Pema Gyamptsho and other ICIMOD personnel. Consultants selected for Dr. Mahesh Banskota for Nepal, Dr. Sangay Duba for Bhutan, and Dr. Luo Peng for Sichuan, China, were also present. The next day, we were provided formal official letters to start work of Assessment of SARD-M Policies in the respective Mountainous countries. The project was to be completed by December 31, 2006.

About 720 million people, 12 percent of the world's population, live in mountain regions. Mountains covers 22 percent of the global land surface. In the world's mountainous regions, 80 percent of the population lives below the poverty line and 270 million people lack food security. Mountain areas provide freshwater to half of the world's population. As much as 78 percent of world's mountain area is unsuitable for growing crops. Under the auspices of FAO, local, national and international groups are joining forces to work for sustainable agriculture and rural development in mountain regions. International awareness on the need for a global drive to improve the lot of mountain people was first stirred at the Earth Summit in Rio in 1992. The International Year of Mountains followed in 2002, as did the World Summit on Sustainable Development in Johennesburg. Mountain people are more exposed to poverty, hunger, social or political marginalization and conflicts and are generally behind in development. On the other hand, mountain areas have significant potential and provide a wide range of goods and services to the rest of society.

1. The Policy Assessment on SARD-M in the Hindu Kush-Himalayas

The Policy Assessment on SARD in the Hindu Kush-Himalayas (HK-H) is a part of the three year Project (2005-2007) SARD-M which has been led by the Food and Agriculture Organization (FAO) and aims to support the rural livelihoods of mountain peoples by facilitating the design, review, implementation and evolution of relevant policy packages and institutional processes promoting SARD in mountain regions at global, regional, national and local levels.

This policy assessment seeks to address the first priority of the SARD-M Project: to assess the strengths and weaknesses of mountain policies, including social, economic, institutional and environmental aspects, in relation to Sustainable Agriculture and Rural Development principles.

Guided by the present political challenges, the policy assessments conducted in the framework of the SARD-M Project constitute a contribution to developing the capacity on policy, institutions and processes for SARD-M in the Hindu Kush-Himalayas (HK-H) for decision makers, civil society representatives and local people alike.

In the Hindu Kush-Himalaya context, this task involved partnership between the FAO, SARD-M Project and ICIMOD and four of its member countries - Bhutan, China (represented by Sichuan), India (represented by Sikkim) and Nepal.

The objectives were:

- To build an initial methodological framework to assess the policies and processes for SARD-M in the selected countries of Himalayas and

- ❖ Assess the strengths and weaknesses of the above policies, institutions and processes.

Since I was involved only in the SARD-M study of mountainous Sikkim, this chapter presents the summary of an overall synthesis policy assessments for mountainous Sikkim which provides a more generalized understanding of past development policies, programmes, processes and institutions, etc., with specific focus on strengths and weaknesses of the past interventions and how to address them in the SARD-M context. This discussion hopes to help educate future initiatives and design follow up to the present series of assessments.

Secondly, it presents the major findings or highlights of the assessment by presenting the findings largely in terms of bullet points rather than extended textual description. The summary focuses on the general background and settings of the country to place the studied sector in proper perspective. This is followed by comments on the sector/ subject under review. There again, details of policy processes, institutions are commented upon. The impacts as well as strengths and weaknesses of the interventions are listed. Finally, the lessons and recommended future steps are briefly mentioned.

1.1 The Hindu Kush-Himalayas Context

The greater Himalayan region sustains approximately 150 million people and has major impact on the lives of three times as many people living in the plains and in the river basins downstream. Not is the Himalayan region the world's highest mountain range, it is also the poorest and most complex. The region extends over 3,500 kilometers from Afghanistan in the west to Myanmar in the east, and ranges from the plateau rigions of Tibet and other mountain areas of China in the north to the Ganges Basin of India in the south. The upland watersheds of Asia's eight major river systems - the Indus, Ganges, Brahmaputra (Yarlungtsangpo), Irrawaddy, Salween (Nu), Mekong (Lancang), Yangtse (Jinsha) and Yellow River (Huanghe) – originate in these mountains. The wealth of the Himalaya also lies in its immense diversity of flora and fauna and ethnic groups and languages. There are approximately 55 different mountain ethnic groups in the mountains of China alone, and estimates for the whole region would exceed 300 groups. Despite its rich cultural and biological diversity, a majority of people in this vast mountain region are abysmally poor and vulnerable to environmental, social and economic threats. Some pockets experience eight months of hunger or food deficit in a year. Such threats have allowed for discontent and conflict to simmer, erupting into violence in several areas.

In the past, policy makers neglected mountain areas, resulting in a general lack of understanding of the natural and human processes affecting these mountains and exclusion of mountain peoples from decision-making. The development interventions that were designed were often extensions of plains' solutions that narrowly addressed the symptoms rather than the causes, largely ignoring appropriate opportunities for development. However, the mountains provide a number of opportunities for mountain specific development and conservation that are increasingly providing a basis for reducing poverty and increasing sustainability. Despite the prevailing constraints in mountain areas, there exists immense potential to promote a chain of development activities, which can lead to the total well being of the people of these areas.

1.2 Features of Development Intervention

Before commenting on the specific agricultural and rural development policies in the Mountainous Sikkim and its sensitivities or links to SARD-M, it is helpful to briefly describe the important features of development interventions on HK-H countries, which strongly influence the thinking and actions focused on in SARD-M. These features (both positive and negative) are imbedded in the degree of sensitivity that development policies and programmes have towards the mountain perspective (i.e. the understanding and incorporation of essential elements of mountain specificities in policy decisions and implementation).

The mountain specificities that generally distinguish mountain situations from mainstream (plain focused) situations are: limited accessibility, fragility, marginality, diversity, niche opportunities and human adaptation mechanisms.

In different HK-H countries, the **development interventions** (i.e. policies and programmes) are generally characterized by their

missing a mountain perspective. The issues involved and implications of this are summarized under Table I[1], that outlines the missing elements required for sustainable mountain development in the region.

It should be noted that the policy programme gaps summarized under col. 2 are not uniformly found in all mountain areas of the HK-H region. Accordingly, some interventions are more sensitive to mountain specificities compared to others.

The main point to be emphasized here is that the broad features of development policy interventions vis-a-vis mountain specificities in HK-H countries can help in identifying and reviewing specific policy issues for SARD-M. **The indicative Policy areas** include the followings:

❖ In the context of agriculture: Agricultural development strategies with focus on investment and resource allocation priorities; Food security and resource access; Technological thrust (Research) and transformation of agriculture; Marketing, trade and high pay off options; Place of mountain agriculture in national context; Agricultural Resource base (national resources) conservation, upgrading and usage planning; Land policies and land reforms; Organic farming and forestry-farming links are areas to be focused by development interventions.

❖ In the context of rural development: Rural infrastructural development and other support systems (physical and financial); Poverty and equity issues and priorities; Niche resources and opportunities and approaches to harness the same; Special programmes for rural areas; Human resource development, capacity building and people's participation (including decentralization); Inter-sectoral and rural-urban links (farming, forestry, fisheries, etc.); Future strategies in the context of globalization and sustainable development are important areas of public intervention, with considerable overlap with the ones listed under agriculture.

The Table I is based on the observations and information culled out from various studies carried out by ICIMOD and other agencies as well as governments' planning documents and project reports. See Jodha, N.S. (1997) "Mountain Agriculture", Chapter 14 in Mountains of the World – A Global Priority, (eds) B. Messerli and Jack, D. Ives Parthenon, New York and London.

Table I. Part A: Indicative details of development interventions in HK-H countries with reference to inaccessibility:

Inaccessibility as a Policy-Programme Context	*Broad Attributes and Orientation of Interventions*	*Sustainability Related Consequences/ Implications*
Dimensions a. External links b. Internal isolation/ distances c. Means of communication, movements d. Issues of social access	**Dominant Pattern** 1. Road construction (in all HK-H countries) with primary focus on harnessing niche resources (e.g. hydropower, irrigation, minerals, timber, tourism). 2. Border security roads (in China, India, and Pakistan). 3. Major national highways – as national needs. 4. General disregard of areas not satisfying (1 to 3) and with difficult terrain and scattered small populations. 5. Limited attention to alternatives (ropeways, improved donkey mountain roads, etc.). 6. Little concern for side effects on fragile slopes; technologies for mountain roads. **Emerging Trends:** 7. Rising concern for 'green roads'; slope stabilization and technologies suited for mountain terrains (in Nepal, China). 8. Community pressures and emerging market needs (due to globalization) for better communication and link roads (with donor support in smaller countries). 9. Initiatives promoting Internet-connectivity in various parts of all countries. **Key Constraints:** 10. Lack of appropriate technologies; high costs and lack of resources, and environmental concerns	**Enhanced Flows, Range/ Quality of Options** • Positive side effects (of 1-3) only where ancillary investments/ facilities available (e.g. Himachal Pradesh, India; Karakoram area in Pakistan; Hunnan Province China; major Valley areas in other countries). • Persistent loss of potential opportunities/ options due to (4) • High expectation from (7-9) in enhancing environmentally safe option and opportunities • Rising economic inequalities between accessible and poorly accessible areas. • Persistent unequal highland-lowland economic links due to (4 & 1). **Resource Depletion:** • Frequent and increased landslides, disruptions etc. in most cases due to (6). • Over-extraction of niche resources due to (1).

Part B: Indicative details of development interventions in HK-H countries with reference to fragility

Fragility as a Policy-Programme Context	*Broad Attributes and Orientation of Interventions*	*Sustainability Related Consequences/ Implications*
Dimensions a. Bio-physical fragility (steep slopes, delicate eco-system features) b. Social fragility (delicate institutional arrangements against vulnerabilities)	**Dominant Pattern** 1. Frequent references in policy-planning documents; disregard in actual interventions (e.g. resource intensification/ disturbance promoted or permitted in agriculture, infrastructural development, mining, etc.). 2. Extension of cropping of fragile slopes under local food self-sufficiency/grow more food programmes, etc. (in all countries). 3. Extension of intensive agricultural technologies (disregarding diversification-led resource conservation/regeneration); promotion of intensive cash cropping on better lands pushing staple crops to steeper slopes. 4. Over grazing, over extraction of NTFPs and other products of fragile areas. 5. Disregard of traditional institutional arrangements and conservation practices by formal administrative, technological, institutional interventions. **Emerging Trends:** 6. Mainly alarmed by negative impacts on downstream areas (e.g. silting of dams), and pressures and incentives built at national/international level, gradual emergence of new initiatives such as bio-sphere reserves, protected areas, rehabilitation of upland slopes, a forestation, etc. 7.Recognition and pleading for community empowerment; decentralization, recognition and use of indigenous knowledge and systems. 8.Recent restrictions on deforestation in most of the countries (preventing cropping beyond certain degree of slope in China). 9.Following of globalization enhanced pressure on high value products/resources (e.g. herbs).	**Enhanced Flows, Range/ Quality of Options** • Temporary/short term increased flows with reduced extent of resource protective options due to (1-4). • Erosion of time tested adaptation options against risks/vulnerabilities (due to 5). **Resource Depletion:** • Rapid, often irreversible erosion of resource base; reduced potential productivity due to (1-5). • Decline of practices/ regenerate resources while using them due to (5). • Emergence of promising new initiatives in terms of resource conservation/ regeneration (6-8). • Herbal extraction rising at alarming rate.

Part C. Indicative details of development interventions in HK-H countries with reference to marginality

Marginality as a Policy-programme context	*Broad Attributes and Orientation of Interventions*	*Sustainability Related Consequences/ Implications*
Dimensions a. Bio-physical marginality (linked to fragility, inaccessibility) offering risky limited production options b. Socio-economic marginalities resulting from (a)vis-a-vis main stream society/ economy reflected by: - Place of mountain areas in dominant national context; invisibility/ disregard of mountain concerns; - Voicelessness/ low capacity and contesting capacity of mountain communities; - Status of indigenous practices/ systems in relation to formal arrangements.	**Dominant Patterns** 1. Reduced physical marginality in limited areas through provision of irrigation, access, new production possibilities (all countries). 2. Recognition of special situation of mountains for liberal funding, subsidies (e.g. to hill states as "special category states" (India); mountain countries as key focal areas under "national poverty alleviation strategies", developed county-mountain county partnership programme", (China); mountains at the centre of national policies of Nepal; mainly indirect approach through "support freedom" to NGOs in Pakistan; renewed development focus on CHT following peace accord in Bangladesh; any national development policy is mountain policy, (Bhutan). 3. Inequity of highland – lowland economic links, not addressed. 4. Despite untied resources and relative freedom/autonomy to hills, development interventions follow patterns of interventions in non-mountain areas (e.g. project components, implementation, delivery system (all countries). **Emerging Trends:** 5. Increased attention to mountain areas (e.g. resource conservation) following downstream concerns (floods, silting of dams, bio-diversity based industries, potential gains from globalization, etc.) in India, China, Pakistan and Nepal. 6. Social-sector services to enhance local capacities, decentralization programmes (using mainstream perspectives) to de-marginalize mountain communities, important NGOs initiatives. 7. Post-Rio global focus on mountain crisis and contributions.	**Enhanced Flows, Range Quality of Options** • Increased options/supplies and reduced risks/ vulnerabilities due to (1) and partly to (2). • Reduced extent of flows and options and related gains due to (3-4). • Local capacity building and other initiatives as yet more formal and limited to be able to initiate socially sustainable processes (6). • Economic globalization likely to accentuate (3), (4) and promote "exclusion" of marginal groups. **Resource base depletion:** • Resource-depleting potential of (3-4). • Possibility of improved resource management due to (5 and 7). • Focus on large-scale environmentally insensitive projects continues despite protests.

Part D. Indicative details of development interventions in HK-H countries with reference to diversity

Diversity as a Policy-programme Context	*Broad Attributes and Orientation of Interventions*	*Sustainability Related Consequences/ Implications*
Dimensions a. Diversity as most central feature reflecting variations in each mountain specificity. b. Heterogeneity at macro-scale (i.e. different ecological/ bio-physical zones). c. Variabilities at sectoral, micro-operational levels in terms of suitability and limitations of specific activities. d. Differing degrees of interlinkages between different mountain specificities. e. Socio-cultural diversities (i.e. ethnic groups; spatial locations/ habitations), differing local perspectives/ practices.	**Dominant Patterns** 1. Broad recognition of the importance of ecological or climate criteria, or of dominant activities-based zones for identifying intervention areas (e.g. high land pastures, horticulture belt, etc. in most countries). 2. Diversities at micro-operational levels, even if recognized, rarely incorporated development activities, i.e. "plurality" of situations ignored while introducing standard type of approaches in keeping with the dominant plain-perspectives of decision makers. 3. The 2 applies to agricultural programmes/ technologies, social services, capacity building, etc. 4. General disregard of diverse nature of mountain areas; mountain communities' diversification strategies ignored; government departments' fragmented structure further reduce the chances of integrated approach to address diversities. 5. Ethnic/cultural entities recognized but development approaches/interventions often bypass them and their knowledge systems. **Emerging Trends:** 6. In some countries, in mostly donor-supported projects, there is a slowly rising awareness about both physical and social diversities of mountains and their application. 7. Pressures and initiatives directed to decentralization, participatory approaches and community empowerment that are conducive to recognizing and responding to diversities. 8. Under globalization, there is likely to be an increased disregard of the imperatives of diversities.	**Enhanced Flows, Range Quality of Options** • Disregard of diversities and diversification at operational levels reduces the range and quality of options, enhances risks and vulnerabilities due to (2-4). • Limited relevance and effectiveness of generalized/ uniform interventions and associated loss of traditionally evolved options due to (2-4). • Positive changes expected from (7). **Resource Depletion:** • Reduced resource conservation, regeneration opportunities promoting unsustainability prospects through (2-4). • Loss of traditionally evolved knowledge/ experiences to harness diversities through diversification approaches due to (5 and 6). • Driving forces/ mechanisms of globalization likely to promote intensification, resource depletion.

Part E: Indicative details of development interventions in HK-H countries with reference to Mountain niche

Mountain Niche as a Policy-programme Context	*Broad Attributes and Orientation of Interventions*	*Sustainability Related Consequences/ Implications*
Dimensions a. Major natural resource endowments: fresh water, hydropower potential, minerals, timber, unique bio-diversity, etc. b. Small niche products (herbs, other NTFPs, etc.). c. Traditional knowledge systems (adaptations to mountain specificities, with rationale usable in modern development policies/ technologies).	**General Patterns** 1. Strong focus on harnessing major mountain niche largely for meeting mainstream/downstream needs, with limited local gains (in most countries). 2. Unrealistic pricing of niche resources, limited compensation to mountains for their resources, environmental services, social displacements and environmental damages. 3. Unequal highland-lowland links unfavourable to mountains. 4. Primary focus on extracting natural endowment with limited man made efforts/investments to strengthen niche. 5. Limited attention to micro-niche products (gathered often by community/poor), huge market-margin in trade; little regulation/restriction on over extraction. 6. Due to promotion/imposition of formal science/management/administration-based interventions, there has been a marginalization and disregard of indigenous knowledge systems that has evolved through people's direct contact with mountain problems and opportunities. **Emerging Trends:** 7. Unless guarded against the above (1-6) tendencies likely to accentuate with economic globalization. 8. Rising NGO and community voices against: over extraction of niche, non-pricing and non-compensation for environmental services and disregard of indigenous knowledge systems. 9. Environmental concerns getting higher place in global agenda (e.g. case of large dams). 10. Local pressures for higher compensation for mountain resources used by the mainstream economy.	**Flows and Range/Quality of Options** • Limited benefits and compensation for mountain communities/ states for extraction of the niche due to (1and 2). • Low gains due to poor compensation, high marketing margin and unfavourable terms of trade due to (3, 4, 5, and 7). **Resources Depletion**: • Over extraction of resources, with little regulation due to (1, 2, 3, 4, and 5). • Loss of valuable indigenous knowledge systems due to (6 and 7). • Globalization may accentuate over extraction of resources and loss of valuable indigenous knowledge systems. • Rising expectation about change in over extraction of resources and loss of valuable indigenous knowledge systems due to (8 and 9).

Part F: Indicative details of development interventions in HK-H countries with reference to Human adaptations

Human Adaptations to Mountain Conditions as a Policy-programme Context	*Broad Attributes and Orientation Interventions*	*Sustainability Related Consequences/ Implementations*
Dimensions a. Traditional institutional and technological practices (e.g. collective risk sharing, common property resources, folk agronomy, etc.) evolved for sustenance under generally harsh and high risk, low productivity environment. b. Focus on diversification, resource regenerative practices/measures. c. Two-way adaptations: adapting demand to local resource capacities and amending resources to demand where possible. d. Regulating demand through population control, migration, etc. regulating resource use by limiting supply.	**General Patterns** 1. No known mainstream policies on this subject, except some donor and NGO-driven projects. 2. Erosion of traditional arrangements/systems due to close integration (at the physical, administrative and economic levels) with the mainstream. 3. Promotion/extraction of modern, formal arrangements for their high performance. 4. Market and state promoted demand driven resource use system replacing the one determined by supply-limitations. 5. Generalized approaches ignoring ethnic, cultural and other specific differences/arrangements. **Emerging Trends:** 6. With market-driven globalization process likely further marginalization of traditional systems. 7. Emerging evidence, advocacy and revival of traditional arrangements by NGOs, etc. 8. Identification of elements of traditional systems for upgrading and incorporation into modern systems, specially technologies and resource management, increasing interest of researchers.	**Enhanced Flows, Range Quality of Options** • Reduced efficacy/ feasibility of traditional measures suited more to low population, subsistence contexts (3-5). • Decline of traditionally evolved institutional defenses against risks/ vulnerabilities (1-5). • Reduced self-controlled, locally-evolved options. **Resource Depletion**: • Disregard/ marginalization of resource regenerative/ protective practices (3-4). • Loss of links between locally relevant measures against diverse mountain specificities (3-4). • Disintegration of organically interlinked/diversified land based activities (1-5).

However, the country teams strongly felt that in the past decade, several of these self-suggestive issues or concerns have been directly or indirectly incorporated in different agricultural and rural development policy-programmes in HK-H countries without formally referring to the SARD-M framework which did not exist at that time. Accordingly, it was agreed to pick up specific agricultural development policy-programmes in each country that tends to reflect on SARD-M components.

1.3 Development history and SARD-M Focus

As SARD-M originated much later than the development processes and structures which were initiated mostly in the 1950s and 1960s, every aspect and approach focused by SARD-M could not find place in the policy-programme assessed by different countries. Besides, the clarity and precision with which issues are identified by SARD-M approach may be missing in different policy-programme components assessed by the country case studies.

In fact, over the past four to five decades, agricultural and rural development efforts (through central planning, etc.) have evolved their own culture (i.e. processes and mechanisms to conceive and design development activities, their financial and institutional support systems) with the state taking up responsibilities of development and promoting top-down approaches with little sensitivity to people's perspectives, skewed structure of development priorities, etc. At the same time, in theory, a number of issues focused by SARD-M such as enhanced agricultural production, poverty reduction, focus on equity and gender concerns as well as natural resource conservation, etc., do find place in the conventional development approaches. However, in terms of genuine priorities and effective implementation some of them (e.g. equity, gender, livelihood complexes, balancing production and conservation needs, etc.) got sidetracked due to narrow growth oriented focus of the interventions.

2.4 Regional Synthesis: Lessons Learned, Recommenda tions and Proposals for Follow-up Activities

2.41 Lessons Learned

The case studies conducted in four countries namely Bhutan, China-Sichuan Province, India-Sikkim State and Nepal show various similarities and differences not only in terms of the specific sectors chosen (Bhutan – Land Use Policies for SARD-M, China – Agriculture and Rural Development Policies for Mountain areas, India-Sikkim – Horticulture as a Driver of Agriculture and Rural Development, and Nepal – The Agriculture Perspective Plan) to reflect on the SARD-M issues focused by the project, but also on the development backgrounds and convergence between conventional development policy interventions and the approaches promoted by SARD framework.

(a) Gaps

While the understanding and adapting to the imperatives of mountain specificities, bio-physical and social conditions of mountain areas is a key to facilitate SARD-M, practically all the countries have neglected to consider mountain specificities in the design and implementation of development interventions. The areas and sectors that are exceptions to this trend have shown better performance in terms of addressing SARD-M.

In spite of the above limitation, the conventional agricultural/ rural development interventions have addressed, at least partially, the concerns of SARD-M. To appreciate the linkages between conventional development policies and approaches and the imperatives of SARD-M framework, it will be useful to understand the conventional development approaches as well as mechanisms and institutional structures.

Due to past practices and backgrounds, the principles of the SARD-M framework are still not fully addressed, despite a visible degree of awareness of the importance of involving primary stakeholders in planning, designing and implementing interventions and the need for a cross-sectional approach. The assessments reveal a continuing weakness in the capacities to act upon the awareness, partly due to the past practices and systems of priority setting and integration of relevant activities and decisions. Of course the inter-country differences are also quite clear when different assessments are compared.

The other important similarities between different case studies, especially with reference to components of SARD-M framework, would include:

- Gaps between planning and implementation of interventions.
- Ad hocism in the shaping and timing of interventions, as opposed to a more systematic approach to policy and programme.
- A low degree of inter-agency coordination in development planning and implementation.

(b) Positive Aspects

While studying the above relatively negative features, what also surfaced is that the past rigidities, lack of coordination and decentralization are diminishing and the use of participatory processes that integrate environmental, economic, social and cultural dimensions of change are gradually gaining ground. This signals an important beginning towards incorporating SARD-M principles more clearly and effectively, i.e. cross-sectoral, integrated, multi-stakeholder and participatory policy formulation and implementation, in agricultural and rural development policies.

While appreciating this healthy change, however, it was also realized as a key lesson that since the macro-level approach to SARD-M, with all its positive attributes, has some operational limitations, it should be supplemented by micro-level initiatives which would help encourage community involvement and ensure focus on a bottom-up approach. This view is supported by some micro-level action research initiatives undertaken by ICIMOD and its partners in the HK-H countries.

2.42 Recommendations of the Project Regional Workshop:

The important – at times overlapping – concerns and suggestions that found frequent mention in assessments and during the SARD-M Project Regional Workshop in the HK-H, attended by senior policy makers, representatives of civil society, international organizations and some bilateral development agencies, are listed below:

(a) Policies

1. Use Gross National Happiness as promoted in Bhutan, a concept of development that shares similar features to the

SARD-M approach, as a possible path for SARD-M once it is put into a concrete usable form.

2. Introduce a more systematic approach to policy formulation using an integrated framework for SARD-M policy programme formulation / promotion / evaluation, rather than depending on largely ad-hoc approaches.
3. Promote awareness, understanding and use of the mountain perspective framework as a tool for designing and implementing SARD-M policies, and for identifying priority areas and groups.
4. Give higher priority to human resource development, equity and women's issues to make SARD-M policies more inclusive.
5. Develop effective and equitable market links (especially with the lowland economy) to ensure developmental gains for mountain people.
6. Focus greater attention on the less-explored issue of supplementing macro approaches with micro-level initiatives and their up-scaling.

(b) Institutions

7. Enhance capacities and coordination of public sectoral agencies/departments dealing with SARD policy making and implementation as an important requirement for SARD-M.
8. Empower mountain people through education, strengthening bargaining capacities and needed autonomy to enhance SARD-M.
9. Reduce duplication and turf-wars through functional coordination and complementaries between different agencies including government departments.

(c) Processes

10. Create a comprehensive database and analytical studies to assist sound and integrated policy making for SARD-M.
11. Enhance interactions between stakeholders at different levels to better balance top-down and bottom-up approaches and processes required to promote SARD-M.

12. Reform institutions to enhance local participation in policy making / implementation, implying genuine decentralization.
13. Upgrade local/grassroots level awareness and capacity building to improve involvement of local stakeholders / communities in policy-programme formulation and implementation through a bottom-up approach.
14. Rationalize resource allocation and investment priorities for mountains *vis-a-vis* lowland economies, with clear understanding of mountain specificities.
15. Improve resource mobilization to reduce donor-dependency and harness public-private complementarities in promoting SARD-M.
16. Strengthen mutual sharing and systematic synthesis of past development / policy intervention experiences and build the future approaches based on successful experiences to make the SARD-M approach more dynamic and effective.

2.43 Proposals for Follow-up Activities

The country reports as well as the regional workshop deliberations identified a range of follow-up actions at regional, national and global levels. The workshop participants prioritized these activities to be taken up as follows:

(a) Regional Level:

- Build stakeholders' capacity at different levels of government in policy processes including formulation, analysis, negotiation and advocacy;
- Identify and put into operation methodologies/approaches for policy formulation that integrate micro-level issues and concerns into macro-level policies;
- Conduct more in-depth institutional analysis in all four countries to identify mechanisms to make policy development and advocacy more inclusive;
- Empower mountain people in the identification of problems and issues and in negotiating skills;
- Sensitize local government officials, elected bodies, civil

societies, lobby groups and farmers' cooperatives in understanding and promoting good SARD-M policies;

- Establish mechanisms for experience sharing in the region particularly in the replication of successful enterprises based on niche mountain products;
- Facilitate south-south exchange of expertise in various mountain development fields and enterprises;
- Establish a virtual network for sharing experiences, views and concerns on mountain issues;
- Build the future approaches based on successful experiences to make the SARD-M approach more dynamic and effective.

(b) National Level

(i) Bhutan:

- Conduct further studies on land markets, taxation and administration systems as an essential input towards developing and implementing a more holistic land use policy and an equitable land reform agenda;
- Assess the capacity building needs of elected officials and local governments and develop and implement a training programme (Duba, Sangay, 2006: SARD-M Policy Assessment in Bhutan).

(ii) China – Sichuan Province:

- Conduct further study to assess policy making and implementation processes in Hengduan ranges;
- Conduct a Sichuan provincial level consultation workshop (with participation from central government agencies) to discuss the findings of the assessment (the consultation workshop was not carried out before the regional workshop) (Peng, Luo 2006: SARD-M Policy Assessment in China - Sichuan).

(ii) India – Sikkim State:

- Identify and document successful horticulture-related

enterprises and establish cooperatives and groups for up-scaling production and marketing;

- Conduct a study to assess land tenure, inheritance and fragmentation issues and propose options for their resolution.
- Conduct a detailed feasibility study for "going organic", which is the adopted policy of the State, identifying potential products as well as measures to tackle constraints and barriers (Subba, Jash Raj 2006: SARD-M Policy Assessment in India – Sikkim).

(iv) Nepal

- Study the opportunities for adopting organic farming under the framework of the Agricultural Perspective Plan;
- Study the impact of the removal of fertilizer subsidies with particular reference to the implications for food security (Banskota, Mahesh, 2006: SARD-M Policy Assessment in Nepal)

(c) For the SARD-M Project at a Global level:

The list of indicative concerns and associated action presented in the preceding sections, though important are numerous to facilitate concrete steps. Hence, to enhance their operational use some integration of issues prioritization is necessary. An effective way to attempt prioritization is to look at the issues from multiple but relevant perspectives or lenses (e.g. stakeholder lens, institutional lens, environmental lens, public-private partnership lens, macro-micro complementary lens, etc.).To achieve this, the following steps could be recommended:

- Promote action on operationalisation of SARD-M framework to help enhance planning and implementing capacities and participation of stakeholders at different levels. This could include approaches to incorporate mountain specificities and practical ways to balance bottom-up and top-down approaches, a need voiced by all case studies and workshop recommendations.
- Approaches and measures to enhance awareness and capacities of communities to participate and contribute to SARD-M at local and higher levels.

- Using inter-country experiences, help in developing practical approaches and tools to promote better inter-agency coordination to design and implement SARD-M interventions.
- Recognising the critical role of emerging environmental (like energy, bio-diversity, etc.) and socio-economic (like community-voices, market processes, technological possibilities) factors/drivers in SARD (ICIMOD 2006. Website: http://www.icimod.org and http://www.fao.org/sard/sard-m).

3. SARD-M Policy Assessment in India (Sikkim):

Since I was Consultant for Sikkim State, a summary of the assessment is also presented for Sikkim study in this chapter.

3.1 The Setting: Indian Himalayas and Sikkim:

The case study introduces Sikkim by profiling the Indian Himalaya region and the comparative status of Sikkim. It provides a broad understanding of the situation of different hill states in India vis-a-vis SARD-M. Important aspects of the setting include the following:

- Broad overview of Himalayan states (11+Nos) of India and position of Sikkim supported by statistical information.
- With the exception of Himachal Pradesh and a few other pockets, large parts of the mountain region are less developed compared to most parts of the country.
- Agricultural crops and horticultural crops in hills have lower productivity compared to plains. Hence there is no food self-sufficiency through domestic production in hill states.
- Yet, the area under food crops is declining due to a shift towards cash crops and horticulture.
- All hill states have heavy dependence on central assistance (as high as over 90% of the development budget).
- Sikkim, the newest and one of the smaller states, is no exception to the above though it has several unique features that make horticulture as an important sector to help in SARD-M.

3.2 Specifics about Sikkim:

Sikkim, a small state in the eastern Himalaya constitutes 0.22 percent of the geographical area and 0.05 percent of the population of India. Rural population constitutes 89% of the total population. The state has about 15.68% cultivable area out of the geographical area of 709,600 hectares. Per capita availability is 0.12 ha of net cultivated area and 0.60 ha of forest area. Land distribution is skewed with small and marginal farmers (less than 2 ha) comprising 70% of farmers but holding only about 28% of the operational area, while 30% of other farmers (semi-medium, medium and large) hold 72% of the operational area. Most small and marginal farmers engage in agriculture as sharecroppers, planting crops of landowners' choice. Land ceiling laws of 1977 and 1978, are still awaiting enforcement. Sustainable livelihood of a family of 6-7 members requires at least 2 ha cultivable area in sloped hills. Population has increased from 406,457 members in 1991 to 540,851 in 2001 and this growth is also likely to accentuate further the land distribution in Sikkim.

Among Himalayan states, Sikkim has the highest percentage of people below the poverty line (36.6%) and the highest percentage of undernourished people (57%) against the country's 26.1% and 35% respectively. The slopping lands are three to four times less efficient in comparison to the plains in meeting the caloric and protein needs of their populations and sustain only three to four persons and one cattle head per hectare per annum through crop intensification and diversification, versus nine to ten persons in a plain land. Thus, diversification of subsistence agriculture to high-value horticulture and livestock is on the rise. Fruits, vegetables, floriculture and spice crop other than large cardamoms are cultivated in horti-agri farming systems.

The State and Central Governments have undertaken a number of measures to address problems associated with inaccessibility, fragility, and marginality such as: improving road and telephone connectivities; improving the state's natural resources and regulation of its uses through low intensity and high stability land uses, diversification involving a mix of high and low intensity land uses, a mix of production and conservation measures with low cost, local resource generation, recycling, regulated use, dependence on nature's processes, and collective measures, different norms for investment to take care of high overhead costs and focusing on vulnerable areas, and people, and their demarginalisation. At the same time, the State has also taken measures to harness the comparative advantages of its mountains (cultural and biological diversity, niche markets, and human capital), and interlinked diversified production and consumption activities differentiated temporally and spatially for fuller use of environment; need diversified and decentralized interventions to match diversity and harness hydropower and develop ecotourism.

3.3 Horticulture in Sikkim

Horticulture is a livelihood option with high economic viability and environmental sustainability. Horticulture covers 34% gross cropped area and contributes to 83% of net income from crops in Sikkim. The range of climatic conditions is favourable for a variety of fruits, flowers, tubers crops, vegetables, aromatic plants for domestic use and export. Important interventions supporting horticulture are the followings:

- Sikkim was declared an organic state, enhancing the market value of Sikkim agricultural products.
- Central Ministry of Commerce approved an agri-export zone covering horticultural products.
- There are investments in improving access, market, energy and communications to help development including horticulture enterprises.
- Several anti-poverty programmes are covering small producers, etc.
- The focus on "eco-tourism based green policy" is affecting all developmental activities.
- A policy guideline from Central Planning Commission (1980) on land use is implemented, concentrating horticulture, agri-horticulture, agro-forestry on slopes from 33% to 50%.

- In 1975-76, the Regional Concept of Agricultural Development (specialization) was adopted to harness comparative advantage of crops/horticulture in different agro-climatic regions and sub-regions.
- In 1996, a full-fledged Department of Horticulture was carved out from Agriculture Department.
- In 2004, a policy resolution was passed for harnessing potential of horticulture and cash crop development in Sikkim.

3.4 Interventions relating to concerns and thrusts of SARD

- The Sikkim Agricultural Land Ceiling and Reforms Act 1977 and its amendment in 1978, not yet enforced.
- The Agricultural Produce Marketing Act 1993, amended in 2005, and enforced.
- The Sikkim Panchayat Act 1993, to promote decentralization and local participation in development planning and implementation enforced.
- Implementation of the National Agricultural Insurance Scheme.
- Passing of bills in 1997 controlling non-biodegradable garbage for environmental health.
- Temporarily prohibiting cutting, lopping and collection of selected endangered plant/shrub/tree species.
- In 2001, release of two historical documents namely "Human Development Report" and "Sikkim People's Vision" indicating the status and lessons for the future.

3.5 Institutional arrangements

- At higher level or national level, both in terms funding (e.g. central grants) and technical or advisory inputs (including recommendations of high power expert communities for production, marketing and planning, etc.), the key part of the industrial structure is the central government.
- At state level, the provincial government, and its multiple

departments develop policies and programme both in keeping with central advice and plans or develop independent initiatives for central assistance and input.

- Though focused on local circumstances (i.e. needs and state's comparative advantage), the policy-programme processes are top-down and do not involve local communities.
- The policy-programmes are guided by positive intentions, but their information and analytical base is not strong.
- For addressing the above problem, the involved agencies are not fully equipped in terms of skills, information and capacities.

3.6 SARD-M: Field verification and analysis

Micro-level verification of situations (though questionnaires and involving mainly small and marginal farmers) of policy-programme interventions revealed the following:

- Farmers manage their livelihood through cultivation of slopped lands (55%), diversification to high-value horticulture (40%), livestock and off-farm activities (50%).
- About 90% of farmers used farmyard manure and rural compost; 40% of farmers trying organic alternatives for their crops.
- Due to ban on grazing in protected/ reserved forests, farmers are managing fodder and fuel needs from their own lands.
- Trend is towards high-yielding milk animals and stall-feeding rather than open grazing.
- Access to services is easier now but the facilities for marketing and processing is poor, affecting diversification towards horticulture/high value crops.
- Pace of village/community development has increased with government policy of decentralization and devolution.
- Farmers have positive response to government's policy decisions, e.g. promotion of horticulture (44%); ban on grazing in forest lands (35%); promotion of organic farming

(48%) and floriculture (27%); promotion of village tourism (24%); establishment of agri-export zones (25%).

- Farmers have adopted a regional comparative advantage based crops for high returns, specially horticulture and vegetable farming.

3.7 Positive impacts of policy-programme interventions

- Diversification led to the transformation of subsistence agriculture towards high-value crops/horticulture.
- Per capita income increased and population below the poverty line declined.
- Both overall and female literacy rate increased.
- Access to infrastructure – road, post office, and electricity increased.
- Human development index and gender development index improved.

3.8 Gaps and weaknesses

- Continued excessive dependence on development grants from the central government.
- At times, conflict between central government and state government regarding programmes and priorities.
- Interventions in keeping with imperatives of mountain specificities are weak and inadequate.
- Often – long gap between formulation of policies and their enforcement.
- Marketing links and processing facilities for high value products are weak and inadequate.
- Capacities of grassroot level workers, communities and government departments do not match with tasks required for SARD-M.

3.9 Recommendations

Future steps should be focused on harnessing and strengthening the positive aspects covered by (3.07) and address the weaknesses indicated under (3.08). In particular, the following may be indicated:

(a) Policies:

- Most of the development activities carried out in Sikkim is quite sensitive to constraints and opportunities in mountain areas, but a more systematic understanding and harnessing of mountain specificities should encouraged.
- Effective and equitable market links should get higher priority.

(b) Institutions:

- Building local capacities (resources, information and skill improvement) to undertake SARD-M (Subba, J. R. 2006; http://www.fao.org/sard/sard-m).

Selected References

Alle, Santosh (2003). *Magar Jatiko Itihas ani Sanskriti Sikkim Ko Sandarbhama*, Gangtok, Sikkim.

Anderson, B. and Afonso, J. C. (1990) (eds). H. Heras - Indological Studies. Pub.Promilla & Co. New Delhi.

Banskota, Mahesh (2006). SARD-M Policy Assessment in Nepal. Draft report submitted to ICIMOD/FAO, Kathmandu/ Rome.

Bhadra, Madhumita (1992). Sikkim – Democracy and Social change. Minerva, India.

Charles, Darwin (1964). On the Origin of Species. Atheneum, New York.

Chemjong, I.S. (1948/2003). History and Culture of Kirat People. Kirat Yakthung Chumlung, Kathmandu, Nepal.

Diamond, Jared (1997). Guns, Germs, and Steel; The fates of Human Societies. Pub.W.W. Norton & Co. New York.

Duba, Sangey (2006). SARD-M Policy Assessment in Bhutan. Draft Report submitted to ICIMOD/FAO, Kathmandu/ Rome.

Foning, A.R. (1987). Lepcha my Vanishing Tribe. Chyu-Pandi Farm, Kalimpong.

Heras, H. (1942). Journal of Bihar and Orissa Society, 28: 113-120.

Hooker, J.D. (1855). Himalayan Journals: Notes of a Naturalist. Vol. I: pp123-124. Pub. Today & Tomorrow's New Delhi.

Howell, F. Clark (1973) (ed). Early Man. Pub. Time-Life Books, New York

ICIMOD. (2006). Project for Sustainable Agriculture and Rural Development in Mountain Regions (SARD-M): Assessment of SARD-M Policies in the Hindu Kush-Himalayas – Sum mary (www.fao.org/sard/sard-m).

Jodha, N.S. (1997) "Mountain Agriculture", Mountains of the World – A Global Priority, (eds) B. Messerli and Jack, D. Ives Parthenon, New York and London.

Johanson D. and Edey, M. (1981). Lucy: The beginnings of hu mankind. Pub. Simon & Schuster Paperbacks, New York.

Karuna Devi Smarak Dharmaguthi (1996). Newa: Barna Lipi ra Bhasa Prichya.

Limboo, R. B. (1989) (ed). *Lipi Sangalo*. Gangtok, Sikkim

Lovejoy, C.O. (1980). Hominid Origins: The role of Bipedalism. Pub. in Am. J. Phys., Anthrop., Fer. 1980: 52-250.

Muley, Gunaker, (1972). *Akchher Katha*. Pub. Ministry of Infor mation and Broadcasting, Government of India.

Peng, Luo (2006). SARD-M Policy Assessment in China. Draft report submitted to ICIMOD/FAO, Kathmandu/Rome.

Pfeiffer, John E. (1969/1972). The Emergence of Man. Pub. Harper & Row, New York.

Plaisier, Heleen (2005). A brief introduction to Lepcha orthography and literature. Bulletin of Tibetology: 41(1). Namgyal Insti tute of Tibetology, Gangtok, Sikkim.

Rahul, Krityanon (1952). Buddha Sanskriti, Kolkota.

Risley, H.H. (1894). Gazetteer of Sikkim. New Delhi.

Sacks, David (2003). The Alphabet. Pub. Arrow, U.K.

Sahaya, Sivswarup (1977). *Bharatiya Puralekhon Ka Adhyan*. Pub. Motilall Banarashidass, Delhi.

Siegen, Halfdan (1967). The Lepcha culture and religion of the Himalayan people. Part-I, Copenhagan, pp.29.

Sprigg, R.K. (2005). Shedding some light on the History, Language and Literature of the Lepchas. Mani Printing Press, Kalimpong.

Subba, B.B. (2004). Samjhanaharu. Pub. Janpakchha, Gangtok, Sikkim.

Subba, B.M. and Subba, J.R. (1994) Cries Unheard. Pub. ASKLCA, Gangtok, Sikkim.

Subba, J.R. (1984). Agriculture in the Hills of Sikkim. Pub. Sikkim Science Society, Sikkim

Subba, J.R. (1995). Vegetable crops of the Himalayan Region.

SYMS, Gangtok, Sikkim.

Subba, J.R. (1999). Limboos of the Eastern Himalayas with special reference to Sikkim, SYMS, Gangtok, Sikkim.

Subba, J.R. (2001). Indigenous Farming Systems of Sikkim Hills and Perspective Planning. ICAR Research Complex for NEH Region.

Subba, J.R. (2002). Biodiversity of Sikkim Himalayas. SYMS, Gangtok, Sikkim.

Subba, J.R. (2002). History and Development of Limboo Language. SYMS, Gangtok,
Sikkim.

Subba, J.R. (2004). Mahatma Sirijunga Singthebe – The Great Social Awakener. SYMS, Gangtok, Sikkim.

Subba, J.R. (2006). SARD-M Policy Assessment in Sikkim(India): Horticulture is an economically viable and environmentally sustainable driver of socio-economic development in moun tainous Sikkim. Study Report Submitted to ICIMOD/FAO, Kathmandu/Rome.

Subba, J.R. (2008). History, Culture and Customs of Sikkim. Gyan Publishing House, New Delhi.

Vansittart, E. (1896). Notes on Nepal. Pub. Asian Educational Services, New Delhi.

Index